The story of the Amersham & District Motor ~~~~~~~~ Ltd.

DEDICATION

This book is dedicated to the memory of Harvey Joiner a~~~~~~~~~~~~~~~~~~~~ng a youthful prank around a moving Amersham & District bus in the ~~~~~~~~~~~~~ i Ley Hill. It was whilst researching this story for a village newsletter that 1 ~~~~ .ed to unearth a wealth of unpublished information about a very interesting local busine~~ rise.

FOREWORD – DAWN OF A NEW ERA 1919

The Amersham & District Motor Bus & Haulage Company became a much loved local institution in 14 short years from 1919. Until now very little has been written about the company that started the first regular motor bus services in Chesham and Amersham, expanding out to serve most of the villages and hamlets for miles around. The effect of offering relatively inexpensive motorised transport to the local community was profound and this book provides several first hand accounts of how people took to the new service, we even learn of a couple who married after meeting on an A&D bus. It is hoped the book captures much that was important to the staff and public from the Company's operations. Sadly the prospect of now finding anyone alive with first hand knowledge of working for A&D is extremely remote but the accounts drawn upon do allow us a good insight into the organisation.

The dawning of a motor bus service was not initially welcomed by everyone, some loved the old ways with horse and carriage, others worried more about the damage to road surfaces, noise and dust, but in the end most realised that huge progress was taking place. The Amersham and District (A&D) bus company took to the highway of history and became a reasonable sized local employer and, most importantly, a reliable conveyor for a great number of residents needing to get to work, shop or simply visit people and places.

Amazingly most of the Company's original Minute Books have survived and along with local newspaper reports it has been established the company was formed by a syndicate of investor entrepreneurs who saw the end of The Great War as an opportunity to start this new business. The founders initially had three main ideas to explore, they wanted to:-
1) Operate a motor haulage company.
2) Offer tours in The Chilterns in charabancs.
3) Create a new network of local bus routes to link areas of 10,000 or more in population.

The cessation of hostilities saw an abundance of army lorry chassis coming onto the market, these could be purchased and put to work very quickly with either lorry beds, charabanc or bus bodies. The army had gone to war with 1,000 lorries and now had over 33,000, most of which were surplus to requirements.

Establishing the business was far from easy, raising initial capital was an uphill battle, profits were hard to come by and vehicle reliability a costly lesson. Amazing changes in vehicle design occurred during the company's short period of activity. From early echoes of stage coaches through to buses of more box-like construction and on to the style of vehicle that eventually saw service into the 1960's and, in some cases, beyond. The chassis also developed, achieving lower ground clearances, moving away from passengers virtually needing to climb a short ladder to board. Some employees initially suffered, having to drive vehicles whilst sitting in the open and even having to repair them at the roadside, should they breakdown. No interior heaters would also cause discomfort for customers in winter but they would enjoy lovely fresh air from wide opening windows in summer.

A lot happened in these 14 years that changed the face of The Chilterns, developing it into the much visited area that it still is today.

About the Author

I trust I don't have to apologise, but this is my first book, so why one on a transport related subject? Well I think it is in the genes. To a degree I explained in the dedication how I came across the material on which to base the narrative, however, the transport related enthusiasm may be passed down from great-grandfather and grandfather who were a locomotive engineer and life long worker on the Underground respectively.

As a toddler my parents wheeled me down to see the last tram run along Streatham High Road. A little later we moved to Kenton near Harrow and it wasn't long before I realised that the buses on the 230 route at the end of our road were different; double-deckers with very odd bench-seats upstairs each holding four passengers. The single-deckers that ran from Edgware Station out to Arnos Grove taking us to see my Nan were so quaint; I named them the "Nanny Bus". Years later I would learn they were London Transport class RLH and TD vehicles respectively. However, my all time favourites were the trolleybuses that ran down the Edgware Road, they did take me to the Christmas party at my Dad's office near Staples Corner so that may have egged on my excited disposition.

On starting secondary school I came across fellow pupils who were avid "bus spotters" and, for about 18 months, I joined their ranks. The scrap-yard for trolleybuses at Colindale was a magnet for souvenir hunters and the freedom of Rover bus passes opened a whole new world to me. It was short lived, with pop culture and the opposite sex eclipsing most other things, so another world beckoned and a bus became a bus and a train a train once again. However, in 1982 I noticed a huge gathering of preserved vehicles at the London Transport garage in Amersham. Taking my wife and 2 year old daughter along, I found that the vehicles of my youth were already seen as nostalgic relics from a past era. A nostalgia that I went on to pigeon hole for another 30 years until I retired and started researching this book.
Neil Lamond, Ley Hill, Chesham. May 2017.

PLEASE NOTE

Throughout the text of this book prices are given in pre-decimal currency figures. For the benefit of those born without experiencing pounds, shillings and pence, I offer some simple guidelines.
The pound has remained the same, albeit worth a fraction today of what it was in the 1920's. The pre-decimal pound was divided into 20 shillings, thus making a shilling worth 5p in today's money; therefore a 10 shilling note would equal our 50p coin. Each shilling was worth 12(d) pennies. Pennies themselves were sub-divided into halves and quarters (known as halfpennies and farthings). Prices were generally written as follows:- £20/12/6 means 20 pounds 12 shillings and six pence. With no pennies in the price it would be written as £20/12/-. If you saw just 1/6 for a price that meant one shilling and sixpence.

CONTENTS

Page

Cover illustration: This imaginary scene of Amersham & District's 1925 Dennis no. 9 dropping off passengers to watch and play golf at Ley Hill Common was commissioned for the book cover and expertly painted by Mary Casserley from Berkhamsted. See more of her remarkable work at www.marycasserley.co.uk.

First published in 2017 © Hawkes Design & Publishing Ltd – www.hawkesdesign.co.uk
ISBN: 978-09554707-9-0

ACKNOWLEDGEMENTS

I am deeply indebted to a number of organisations and very kind people for their help in compiling this book.

The Amersham & District Motor Bus Society, particularly their President, **John Hutchinson** who has become a friend following his insistence that I convert my early research into this book. Dates for the Society's "Running Days" are listed at www.amershammotorbussociety.co.uk.

John Hutchinson, Born in Isleworth, moved to Tylers Green in 1970, started working for London Country Bus Services out of Amersham the following year. John's career in public transport spanned 40 years during which time he amassed a huge collection of material relating to the history of local buses and those who worked on them. His enthusiasm sparked bus garage open-days and a dedicated society to the running of vintage vehicles for all to enjoy. John fondly remembers **Wilf Brackley** and **Ernie Revel** who actively supported his gathering of photographs and memorabilia from the days of the early Amersham bus services.

The family of **Will Randall**.

The family of **Jim Chapman**.

Mr Jim Hounslow (son of **Percy Hounslow**).

Alan B Cross, who truly went out of his way to help the project.

A.D.Packer, who similarly gave me assistance.

Ian Garland, a friend and life-long researcher.

The Kithead Trust, particularly Philip Kirk.

The Omnibus Society, particularly Alan Mills who sadly died before we went to print.

The Transport Ticket Society.

The Francis Frith Collection.

The Amersham Museum.

The London Transport Museum, staff at Acton and Covent Garden.

The London Bus Museum, particularly Brian Jones.

The Buckinghamshire Centre for Studies.

The Bucks Examiner

Rita Richardson and Phyllis Clarke (Harvey Joiner's sister) for their photographs.

Ron Atherton, Paul Lacey, Peter Hawkes, Keith Fletcher, I Lamond, R Sanders, Barry Wilkinson, Paul Dodge, Michael Rooum.

COPYRIGHT

THE VISION OF MOTOR BUS SERVICES

Drawing N Lamond after Patterson

"White roads innocent of oil and petrol …… where the horse was king," was the way Laurie Lee described his childhood village in his early 20th century best selling book "Cider with Rosie". Our small Buckinghamshire villages un-deformed by telephone boxes, zebra crossings and yellow lines had remained largely unaltered for a hundred years or more. Now, following the end of The Great War, the demise of the horse drawn era in the countryside was gathering pace. Train services had been developing for over 70 years but it was still the good old horse and carriage that conveyed people on their journeys to the stations or out to the smaller villages of the Chilterns. The tuneful sound of the slender copper coaching horn was to be replaced by the "honk-honk" from the brass, rubber bulb activated, trumpet horns fitted to new omnibuses. For most, until now, journeys beyond walking distance were a rare occurrence, almost everything in their lives happened locally. However, times were changing rapidly, greater employment opportunities were farther afield and the lure of new horizons beckoned. The era of the petrol engine was about to take off in the sleepy hollows of Amersham and Chesham. New sounds of motion would fill the streets that the stage coaches had departed. However, nostalgia for the day of the horse was slow to wane, in fact even in 1928, following the laying of a new tarmac road west of High Wycombe, the Old Berkeley Coach was re-instated for a month of commemorative journeys between London and Oxford. Each one taking 8 hours, it was reported in the Telegraph newspaper as the spic and span horses and coach against the "Stinkin Moty Car," such was the distain in some circles for newer forms of transport. The horse however, would be used in ever diminishing numbers as a commercial transporter and had pretty well disappeared inside 30 years.

Prior to The Great War, motor bus services had spread north-west out of London, reaching Harrow and Watford. However, the outbreak of hostilities meant a reduction in these outer lying services as buses were requisitioned to become troop carriers or converted to lorries for the war effort. The former bus owners often being left with bus bodies to store, as only the chassis were taken.

By 1919 limited motorised lorry and charabanc services were available in the Amersham and Chesham area but a regular timetabled motor bus service was an entirely new proposition. It was reported in the Bucks Examiner (February 1919) that Mr R V Dell writing from H M Gun Wharf, Chatham along with the County Motor Garage Company of Gerrards Cross have both applied for licences to run services. R V Dell wanted to run a bus and char-a-banc service taking in High Wycombe, Beaconsfield, Amersham, Chesham and Berkhampstead (sic). County Motor Garage wanted its licence to run an omnibus service between Amersham, Chalfont St Giles, Beaconsfield, Seer Green and Gerrards Cross. Both claimed much anticipated demand and benefit to the community. The newspaper reported that in discussion the Council said there were feelings that it "was undesirable that there should be heavy motor traffic over the roads, with resultant damage, without the Council having control, although in the interest of the public it was desirable to encourage such conveyances." The matter was left with the Clerk to deal with as he saw fit; hardly a ringing endorsement for the applicants' modern plans. Nothing further is reported to say if either application was granted. In the same edition a member of the public wrote to the editor in support of the idea of a motor bus service connecting Chesham with Gerrards Cross, Berkhamsted and High Wycombe but warns the Council to keep an eye on the considerable wear and tear on the roads.

The following week another letter to the editor gives support to the general idea of motor buses but says "the type of motor bus suitable for these hills is by no means the double-decker, but a covered-in type after the fashion of Messrs Fosters motor charabanc." Fosters ran a motor sales and repair business in Chesham. The writer further says "we need tarmac roads otherwise we will be blighted by mud and dust".

Clearly, on seeing these new applications there were members of the public who shared the Council's concerns. On 14th March 1919 a letter published in the same local paper claimed first hand experience of new motor bus services appearing on the roads. The writer said "*I regret to learn that motor buses may be running to and from Chesham during the coming summer. I have previously lived in two districts nearer London that have been invaded by them, and their advent was a definite disturbance to the cleanliness, quietness and beauty of the districts*". The writer went on to complain about the "*noisy red, advertisement-splashed juggernauts*" causing untold noise, pot holes, dust in summer and mud in winter. If they are to run, can the roads be made up properly first and the buses not covered in "*music hall and quack medicine advertisements?*" It seemed this writer was certainly anticipating the arrival of double-decker buses as damage to overhanging trees is also mentioned.

On the 21st March a third application to start running motor bus services was reported. This time it was from E.C. Miles and Co. of Amersham who applied to run a service between Chesham and Amersham and on to High Wycombe. In this case the local council found no objection to the company running these services on the area of roads covered by their jurisdiction.

Mr Edward Curling Miles ran the garage at the rear of The Griffin, Amersham and was to become the Company Secretary for the newly formed Amersham and District Motor Bus and Haulage Company. Clearly plans to start running the company gathered pace following the Council's positive decision. In May a succession of announcements from the company appeared in the Bucks Examiner. Mr Miles and a syndicate of local businessmen had already decided to invest in the business. Later in the year, when the size of the syndicate was disclosed it gave some indication that they might have been aiming to create a business on a largish scale.

There were no new buses or lorries available to buy at this time as production had not started up again following the end of war. However, there was an excess of army vehicles flooding back to England and these could be purchased and have bodies made to suit requirements. There were also more drivers available who had received tuition in the army and were now returning to civilian life. Some army surplus sales took place at Slough and it is known that Amersham Council bought ex-army vehicles from a site at Richborough.

This line drawing illustrates a typical 3-ton chassis for sale in 1919.
Part of a 1919 advert appearing in the local newspapers.

The syndicate forming Amersham & District Motor Bus & Haulage Co., Griffin Garage, Amersham, licensed BH0157 an AEC 3 ton, 40/50 HP lorry on 15th May 1919 and it was noted in Bucks CC records as being "service colour". Presumably this meant army green colour. On 16th May 1919 a block advertisement in the local press announced "The Amersham and District Motor Bus and Haulage Co. have now opened the Haulage Branch of their business and will contract to remove anything with up-to-date 3-ton lorries. Apply: The Griffin Garage, Amersham. We hope shortly to start our Bus Service but the delay being in getting delivery from the manufacturers."

A 32hp ex. WD Scout chassis subsequently fitted with a bus body and painted green and yellow was licensed BH0158 on 24th May 1919, the day prior to this the same block advert had appeared where the final sentence was replaced as follows:- "The Bus Service will be commenced on Monday next! Times and Fares Issued Later." So the first motor bus serving the towns of Chesham and Amersham started on 26th May 1919. The rich stream of country life that had flowed unaltered for so long was changing; the omnibus would bring the town to the end of the country lane.

The Scout chassis bought by the syndicate had originally been made in Salisbury prior to 1915 when the entire company was requisitioned for war work and all the factory tooling sent to the front. It seems a general rule, that at this time when second-hand chassis were purchased, the new owner would register them in their own county and new number plates would be issued. This practice clearly made the vehicle look newer than it actually was, on paper anyway.

Just four days after the A&D service started a letter published in the local press read as follows:-

"The kiddies have discovered a joy-ride, and it has been a treat this week to see them clambering into and swarming around the motor-bus. It is a new toy to them and the novelty will soon wear off.

But it is by no means a toy to their elders, and great advantage has been taken of the short-trip facilities - through the town and up to Bois Common. The bus considerably facilitates shopping for those living on the Common. With a full service, so that bus makes a more frequent appearance in Chesham and covers the Berkhampstead route, the bus should prove a boon. There have been inquiries this week as to the possibilities of a service to Watford. It would not be an easy one, as the road presents many difficulties between here and Chorley Wood. After that it would be plain sailing".

Also on 30th May 1919, A&D published their first time and fare table. It was reprinted for a few weeks in the Chesham, Amersham and High Wycombe local newspapers.

THE AMERSHAM AND DISTRICT
MOTOR BUS COMPANY.

	A.M.	P.M.	PARES:
Dep. AMERSHAM, Griffin Garage	9.0	2.0	
Queen's Head	9.10	2.30	2d.
Lord Nelson	9.15	2.15	3d. Amersham
Penn Street Church	9.25	2.25	2d. to
Holmer Green, Earl Howe	9.35	2.35	4d. Wycombe
Haslemere, Three Horse Shoes	2.45	2.45	4d. 1/8
Terriers	2.55	2.55	2d.
Arr. WYCOMBE, Falcon Hotel	10.15	3.15	4d.

	A.M.	P.M.	
Dep. WYCOMBE, Falcon Hotel	10.45	4.15	
Terriers	11.5	6.35	
Haslemere, Three Horse Shoes	11.15	4.45	
Holmer Green, Earl Howe	11.25	4.55	
Penn Street Church	11.35	5.5	
Lord Nelson	11.45	5.15	
Queen's Head	11.50	5.20	
Arr. AMERSHAM, Griffin	12.0	5.30	

	P.M.	P.M.	P.M.	
Dep. AMERSHAM, Griffin	12.0	6.0	8.30	Amersham
Amersham Station Hotel	12.7	6.7	8.37 5d. to Nashleigh
Bois Avenue	12.15	6.15	8.45 2d. Arms
Chesham Town Hall	12.25	6.25	8.55 2d. 8d.
Arr. CHESHAM, Nashleigh Arms	12.30	6.30	9.0 1d.

	P.M.	P.M.	P.M.
Dep. CHESHAM, Nashleigh Arms	12.35	7.0	9.30
Chesham Town Hall	12.40	7.5	9.35
Bois Avenue	12.50	7.15	9.45
Amersham Station Hotel	1.0	7.25	9.55
Arr. AMERSHAM, Griffin Garage	1.5	7.35	10.5

SATURDAYS ONLY.
Dep.—The 9.30 p.m. 'Bus leaves at 10.0 p.m. from Town Hall, Chesham.

Through Fare Wycombe to Chesham, 2/4.

SUBJECT TO ALTERATIONS.

May/June 1919 advertisement placed in the local press by A&D

The weekday running shows the service to comprise of two return trips between Amersham and High Wycombe, one in the morning and one in the afternoon with three shorter return trips just between Chesham and Amersham, two in the afternoon and one in the evening. Prices are 8d Chesham to Amersham and 1/8d Amersham to High Wycombe.

The weekday service seems not to offer anyone from Chesham the opportunity to go to High Wycombe for a few hours shopping unless they first walk to Amersham in the morning. This timetable could be operated by one bus. On Saturdays there is one departure from Chesham to High Wycombe for a fare of 2/4d. A ticket (not to size) from that early running of the Saturday bus service is illustrated, although shown here in black and white it has red pricing on a green background, all other text is in black.

Image courtesy of The Omnibus Society

A revised timetable was published on 11th July making some minor changes and the following day the Company licensed BH0193, a second identical Scout bus.

June 13TH 1919 ACCIDENT IN THE VALE: letter to local paper.

"Many townspeople no doubt noticed the handsome motor charabanc which came through Chesham on Tuesday. It was a Rushden vehicle, and the party were "doing" Watford, taking Chesham en route and renewing old acquaintanceship in this town. A most enjoyable trip! But these big vehicles upon the road have their drawbacks. In the Vale, Mr Alfred Gee, who was driving, almost passed the vehicle, but not quite, and a slight "touch" – heavy enough from such a vehicle – swung his trap round, and broke the shafts. There were no personal injuries, fortunately".

An absolutely charming and long letter appeared in the local press on 18th July 1919. The writer is conveying to the community how wonderful the views can be when riding *"up top"* on a bus. Travelling roads long known to the writer from years of foot travel, the new views showed our *"charming surroundings"* of people's gardens, houses and more distant views, better than could be imagined. *"Never did I realise until I got on-top that this particular bit of road had so much to offer."* This letter may lead readers to believe that the new buses running into Chesham and Amersham are double-deckers, however, although not recorded at Bucks CC licensing department the two Scouts are known to have been single deck 26-seaters.

The founders of The Amersham and District Motor Bus and Haulage Co. had always intended to convert the business to be a limited liability company, selling shares to interested parties. They placed advertisements in the local press in September 1919 offering 10,000 shares at £1 each, to be paid by 10/- (Ten shillings is 50p) per share on application and the remaining 10/- on allotment. The money raised was to "purchase the business of The Amersham and District Motor Bus and Haulage Co." The directors of the new company were:- Charles Ivins, Amersham; George Robert Knowles, Amersham; Robert Herbert Brazil, Amersham; Henry Gurney, Penn and William Franklin, 25 Polygon Mews, London W2. Mr E.C. Miles was Secretary, a job he continued to do until a Mr Stone took over in September 1920. At the first meeting of the new board on 28th October 1919 Mr Charles Ivins was appointed chairman. Francis and Howe of Chesham were appointed company solicitors.

Shares in the Company were slow to sell and after a year only 1589 had been taken up, plus 1200 issued to the vendor syndicate members. However, the business was underway, any profit from the first 4 months went to the syndicate and only the 12 months figures to 30th September 1920 were reported in the first set of accounts for the limited company.

The Company advertised a winter timetable on 10th October which they repeated in the local press for a few weeks. The winter weekday timetable cut services down to two daily returns Chesham to Amersham and one return trip to High Wycombe in the afternoon, Sunday services between Chesham and Amersham were also offered. At this time they also advertised a 2 hour 45 minute charabanc round trip to Windsor on 12th October for six shillings. Although not licenced at Bucks CC, the syndicate's first charabanc is believed to have been a Dennis with registration number P3569. We do, however, know from later entries in their minute books that they hired charabancs from Fosters Garage in Chesham or Bucks Mechanical Transport when they had none available of their own.

The first anniversary of the Armistice was 11th November 1919 and King George V issued a proclamation calling for a two minute silence when "all locomotion should cease, so that, in perfect stillness, the thoughts of everyone may be concentrated on reverent remembrance of the glorious dead". It is not recorded if the Board asked for the company's bus to stop at 11:00 am but we can be sure the thoughts of everyone would have been on the dreadful events of war, now just one year behind them.

The A&D Board had selected "The Pride of Bucks" as the name for their proposed fleet of charabancs. Just as famous named ships and trains took people on exotic journeys, so would the A&D vehicles. For many, a trip to Marlow or Windsor and a walk along the Thames would have seemed a world away from their home town or village that they may never before have left. "The Pride of Bucks" name was sign written in a rainbow style arc across the back of the coaches, the main colour of the vehicle's body was listed as grey in Bucks CC licensing records.

"Charabanc" comes from the French for a carriage with benches and these vehicles were exactly that, a lorry chassis with benches seating about 5 across. The really early ones had wooden benches but soon were made more comfortable with full width padded seating.

The Company's original plan was to market charabanc tours via Messrs. Thos. Cook but that seems not to have worked to the directors' satisfaction. The Company gave their charabanc business a kick start at the beginning of 1920 with six months' advertising starting on 23rd January promoting their own "Pride of Bucks" outings weekly in the local press.

A&D weekly advert from 23rd January 1920
Reproduced from the Bucks Examiner

Although the advert says "char-a-bancs" they only had one at this stage. It states a charabanc seated 28 people and trips were ideal for "Bean feasts, school outings and pleasure trips." A "Bean Feast" in those days referred to a trip where the hirer also provided some food and refreshments.

This vehicle is registered P3569 and is probably the first charabanc that A&D used; it was originally rented to A&D by the syndicate. The registration was issued in Surrey prior to WWI. Later this charabanc carried bonnet no. 2, although it was the first that A&D used back in 1919, it was the second one they actually purchased. Photograph taken outside the Kings Arms, Old Amersham. Identical vehicles to this one were advertised at this time by Dennis and sold painted in "Torpedo Grey".
Photo Jim Chapman collection

These photographs show (left) the driver's position on an early charabanc. The handbrake lever operating rods controlling the rear drum brakes; the footbrake operates the same. The brass box below and to the left of the steering wheel feeds a water top-up system for the radiator. (Right) Detail of a carbide operated headlamp fitted to a charabanc; water drops onto blocks of carbide and an ignitable gas (acetylene) is given off which burns at the top of the tube visible in front of the reflector. In the Company's 1921 accounts they list 9/- worth of carbide in stock. The lamps clip on and off from U-shaped brackets fixed either side of the radiator.
Photographs N Lamond

11

The syndicate's total spend on their first vehicles, once bodies were fitted, was not far short of £5000, the Dennis charabanc alone cost £1600. It is worth saying at this point that these buses were pretty much of the very earliest designs for motorised vehicles, bodies were set high off the ground and made of wooden frames. They all ran on solid tyres and would only have had rear braking. The drivers sat on a wood bench seat open to all weathers, main night lighting would be by acetylene (otherwise known as carbide) lamps and sometimes with oil burning side lights. In summer the drivers got covered in whitish dust from the dry roads and in winter, soaked and mud splattered. Life was certainly tough on the buses of 1919, heavy steering and poor braking were two things to contend with but the crew also had to have some knowledge of the mechanicals as it was hoped they could make running repairs in the event of breakdowns. The new fleet would operate from Mr Miles' garage at the rear of The Griffin. He already had a petrol pump and would continue to run his motor and fuel business separately and charge A&D for rent and other services provided.

It seemed that the Scout buses were proving unreliable as on 12th January 1920 the new Limited Company board resolved to accept Messrs Hodson's estimate of £435 for a new bus body interchangeable with the body on the AEC lorry chassis (Hodson as recorded in the minutes may be Hodsdons coachbuilders of High Wycombe mentioned in the 1911 census). This body would convert the AEC lorry into a bus which we later know had 26 seats. A sum of £435 is the equivalent of buying a freehold cottage in Amersham at the time. Simultaneous to fitting the AEC with a new bus body, the original Scout bus (BH0158) was converted into a lorry in order to carry on with the small haulage side of their operations. Furthermore an additional unspecified chassis was then delivered to the Company on Monday 26th April 1920.

No photographs of the Scout buses or the now converted AEC bus have been positively identified in the preparation for this book. However, the body of a very early bus can be partially seen in a 1921 Francis Frith photo of Chesham Broadway. The type of body captured in the picture was a style briefly favoured in the immediate post-war period and retains echoes of earlier designs from horse-drawn buses. The interior would have been fairly basic, there will be no lighting and the ribbed fame of the vehicle's body will be exposed on the insides and roof. The Frith photograph has allowed us to speculate a little and draw a sketch of the full bus. It has what is called a clerestory roof giving extra light and height into the saloon which would have been entered at the very rear of the vehicle up 2 or 3 steps. Given that the photograph is dated 1921 and seemingly taken in summer, there is a distinct probability that it is of the AEC bus BH0157 or an outside chance that it is the remaining Scout BH0193. However, as we will see later the Scout was known to be "off the road" for the summer of 1921 so it seems less likely to be that vehicle.

The newly "Limited" Company certainly needed to raise more money if they were to buy all the vehicles from the syndicate. With share sales remaining poor, in April 1920 it was decided to raise some extra capital by issuing interest bearing (10%) debentures; £4000 worth were advertised nationally and this proved more successful. In the first year though, the Limited Company only went on to buy the AEC and the two Scouts from the syndicate and it was reported in the accounts to 30th September 1920 they paid £3200 for these. The original charabanc, it was agreed, they could continue to use but they must pay the full ongoing monthly loan costs to the Syndicate in order to do so. It is further recorded they still owe the syndicate £1190.

A lovely early photograph of The Broadway, Chesham. Taken in 1921 it shows how quiet the streets could be. On the left hand side we see one of the very first motor buses to ply its trade into the town. A fuller illustration of how this bus would have looked is reproduced below.

Copyright The Francis Frith Collection, reprinted with their kind permission.

This drawing is a representation of one the first buses used by Amersham & District Motor Bus Co. Drawing R Atherton.

An interior view from a solid tyred bus of this period. It clearly shows the design and skills of body builders at this time. The driver sits outside in all weathers, with the merest of canopies over his head. The wooden ribbed framework is fully exposed. In this case the seats are padded but the ride would still have been very harsh on anything but the smoothest of surfaces. Photograph N Lamond

Takings for the year to 30th September 1920 amounted to £3497 but profit was only £32. From the accounts at this time we see that William Franklin was no longer listed as a director, replaced by Mr A C Norman of Bayswater London. It is also worth noting the directors took no money nor expenses. Drivers were paid £6 p.w, the fitter £3/15/- and the garage was rented for £2 a week. Bus drivers needed a licence to drive at this time although they were not tested on their abilities by any authority. They simply bought an annual licence at the Post Office for one shilling and self certified they were fit to drive! In 1919 there were less than 1 million drivers in Britain.

Like any fledgling business, A&D was not without its difficulties, the reliability the Scouts remained poor, such that both were often off the road. During the summer of 1920 the Company had experimented with a new bus route between Uxbridge and Aylesbury, but this did not gain enough public patronage and was withdrawn. A strike in High Wycombe had certainly affected passenger journeys during the past 12 months. In October 1920 driver Philbey was called to account for driving at more than 12 mph and later that month when one of the buses was performing the difficult manoeuvre out from the back of The Griffin into Whieldon Street it knocked over a telegraph pole. The Post Office charged the Company £13/6/8 in damages. However, generally the converted AEC bus performed well and clearly brought in the lions share of the takings. Chepping Wycombe Council had even asked if the bus could stop more frequently and the Board agreed it could stop anywhere if requested.

As the year closed it was agreed with Mr Miles that his employee, Mr Will Randall, would transfer to Amersham & District's employment and become their Management Fitter on a wage of £4/0/0 per week plus 5% of takings over £40.

THINGS DO NOT GO ENTIRELY TO PLAN

The roads around Amersham and Chesham left a lot to be desired when used by these early buses. Being generally of a compacted but loose surface, they were prone to pot holes and as previously mentioned, dust and mud. However, it was reported that 1921 was the year that Buckinghamshire County Council had agreed to tarmac the area's main highways, so the directors and staff should have been rather happy with that news. Also, factoring in the previous year's good regular bus route result, the Board should have had some heightened confidence. On the 10th January 1921 they made an enquiry with Dennis Bros. of Guildford for another (30-seater) charabanc either new or second-hand, they did this despite recently declaring disappointment with charabanc takings. Trying a new approach they decided not to run charabanc tours as before but quoted for party outings on application. They also finally discontinued any arrangements with Messrs. Thos. Cook & Sons. However, they didn't do any advertising in the Bucks Examiner for the entire year and also decided not to renew an advertisement in Metro-Land (the magazine of The Metropolitan Railway). In fact they did not record any decisions on how they would promote their fledgling business. With expansion in mind though, in February, the Board asked the Company Secretary to write to the Council and seek permission for running a service between Chesham and Berkhamsted. They further minuted the acceptance of a quote of £350 from Mr J M Roberts of Shepherds Bush to deliver a charabanc body and mount it on the chassis of the Dennis bus. In March they were advised that this Dennis charabanc, undergoing assembly, required new rear tyres at £7 each, so clearly it was a second-hand Dennis chassis not listed in the Company's stock at the close of accounts five months earlier.

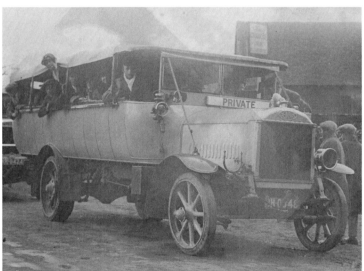

This second Dennis charabanc registered in 1920 as BH0348, the vehicle was first delivered to A&D in May 1920 and was registered as being grey in colour. The minutes are not totally clear on the origins of this vehicle but at the outset it appears to have been bought as a second-hand bus, the charabanc body shown above being fitted by J M Roberts of Shepherds Bush in February 1921. The company then took delivery of it as a charabanc on 23rd March 1921. J M Roberts charge for the work was £350.
Photo W Randall collection

Although unrecorded in the A&D minutes, Bucks CC licensing records show the company had registered a vehicle, BH0348 in May 1920. The "new" charabanc was delivered on 25th March 1921; they now had two charabancs at their disposal. Also in March, Mr Edward C Miles, owner of The Griffin Garage, became a Director of A&D.

Local competition for tours came from Foster's Garage of Chesham who placed a succession of four weekly adverts promoting their "Albatross" charabanc. In July A&D paid Foster's £2 to hire this charabanc, presumably they either had three bookings on that occasion or one of their own charabancs was out of action.

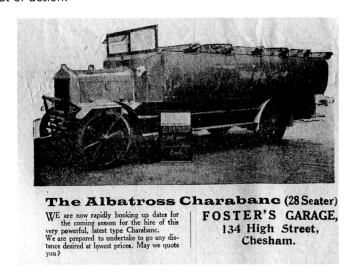

The Albatross Charabanc (28 Seater)

WE are now rapidly booking up dates for the coming season for the hire of this very powerful, latest type Charabanc. We are prepared to undertake to go any distance desired at lowest prices. May we quote you?

FOSTER'S GARAGE,
134 High Street,
Chesham.

1921 Bucks Examiner advertisement for Foster's "Albatross"

Due to continued unreliability, the Scout chassis recently converted to a lorry and now owned for less than two years, was recorded as being sold at auction for a mere £46.

Berkhamsted U.D.C. replied to the Company to say they had no objection to the proposed Chesham to Berkhamsted route.

In August 1921 the Company received a complaint from Mr Abrahams who had bought a year's advertising on two buses and found only one had been running that summer.

Unexpectedly and having only just become a director, Mr Miles died. This must have been shock enough to the Board, but Mrs Miles almost immediately sought to double her husband's garage rent to the Company!

By the end of September they had additionally sold the "old Scout bus chassis", which realised just £49. Both Scout vehicles were listed in the accounts to 30th September 1921 as having caused the company to lose a massive £1665 out of an initial investment of £3200. In the report accompanying these accounts the Board also says they suffered severe competition on its regular bus route and price cutting such that takings fell to £3130, about 10% down on 1920. They now had in stock:- 1 AEC bus, 1 new chassis costing £1190 and 2 charabancs.

16

A&D had initially started enduring competition from the Penn Bus Company in 1920 on the section from Hazlemere to High Wycombe. A further challenge began at the end of August 1921 on the section between Chesham and Amersham, because the National Bus Company had extended its N6 Route out of Watford to take in the two towns.

On 11th October 1921 Bucks CC licensing records show A&D registered a green Dennis lorry (BH8331), it weighed 3 tons 16 cwt. As the lorry was green it possibly indicates they adopted that colour as the brand colour across both bus and haulage operations.

The business has now been running 2½ years and they only have one bus and one route in operation. Will 1922 be better for them?

Well, things did not actually get off to the best of starts with the AEC bus requiring a new engine costing £180; still it had given far better service than the Scouts.

The company employed the periodic services of a ticket inspector (Mr E Cook) who boarded the bus unannounced, but it seems he was pleased to find things running well. Later handed down information indicates that the Amersham & District staff became so trusted by management that they were given free access to take fresh ticket stocks from the stores and their takings were left in allocated individual, but unlocked drawers, with no inspectors employed for some time.

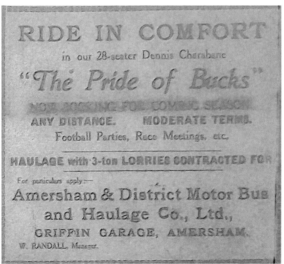

Advertisement placed in the Bucks Examiner February 1922

From early on this year A&D started promoting the hire of their charabancs, on 24th February 1922 their advertisement stated "RIDE IN COMFORT in our 28-seat Dennis Charabanc "The Pride of Bucks". This is the first time we see "W RANDALL, Manager" in print, so since becoming Management Fitter in December 1920 he is now overall Manager of operations. By June 1922 more competition was emerging, with Rickmansworth & District Bus Company starting a service (their No. 2 route) to Chesham via Amersham. The Board now contemplated more passengers being lost on the short but important stretch between these two towns.

In July they finally settled Mr Abrahams' advertising claim, they acknowledged that the second bus (the original Scout) was off the road for the half year ending September 1921 and agreed to refund £20 if he would take advertising rights on the one remaining bus from September '21 – September '23 at £10 per annum.

The company was finally planning a second regular bus route; it would run from Chesham to Slough with 5 departures a day, so another bus would be needed. They ordered a new Oldsmobile chassis for £295 and agreed that C Hodsons (again maybe Hodsdons of High Wycombe) would build a new 14-seat bus body for it. The first where the driver would sit inside and collect fares as well. Later reference to this bus, in Company minutes, tells us it was given the A&D bonnet no.4. The new bus route was advertised in the local press on 4th August 1922, we are also lucky to have a photograph of Chesham Broadway taken shortly after this date and can see the new 14 seat Oldsmobile in the picture.

Photo R East collection courtesy P Hawkes.

Inset is a close up of the bus from this photograph

1922 Oldsmobile 14-seater, BH9306, A&D bonnet no. 4. From this photograph we gain our first look at the company name sign written in white on the side of the vehicle. The full name has been abbreviated by omitting the words "& Haulage." This vehicle appears to be same colour all over, so the yellow that appeared on the original vehicles has been dropped.

AMERSHAM & DISTRICT MOTOR BUS & HAULAGE CO., LTD.

SLOUGH AND CHESHAM

Alteration of Time Table and Route, commencing Wednesday, August 2nd.

CHESHAM TO SLOUGH.

			WEEKDAYS				SUNDAYS				
		a.m.	S.O. p.m.	S.E. p.m.	S.O. p.m.	S.O. p.m.	p.m.	p.m.	p.m.	p.m.	
CHESHAM BROADWAY	dep.	8.10	1.25	2.45	5.0	8.40	1.25	—	—	7.50	Through Fares Chesham to Slough 2s.
Oakfield Corner	"	8.20	1.35	2.52	5.10	8.50	1.35	—	—	8.0	
Amersham (The Chequers)	"	8.25	1.41	3.0	5.16	8.56	1.41	—	—	8.6	
Chalfont St. Giles (The Pheasant)	"	8.34	1.50	3.9	5.25	9.5	1.50	—	—	—	
Chalfont St. Peter (The Church)	"	8.42	1.58	3.17	5.33	9.13	1.58	3.45	5.30	—	
Gerrards Cross Station	"	8.49	2.7	3.26	5.42	9.22	2.7	3.54	5.39	—	Amersham to Slough 1s. 8d.
Stoke Poges (Sefton Arms)	"	9.3	2.21	3.40	5.56	—	2.21	4.8	5.53	—	
SLOUGH {The Clock House / Temperance Hotel}	arr.	9.17	2.35	3.54	6.10	—	2.35	4.26	6.9	—	

		a.m.	S.O. p.m.	S.E. p.m.	S.O. p.m.	S.O. p.m.	p.m.	p.m.	p.m.	p.m.	
SLOUGH {The Clock House / Temperance Hotel}	dep.	9.40	3.0	4.54	6.30	—	—	3.0	4.40	6.30	"Pride of Bucks" 28-seater Char-a-Banc for Hire. Any Distance Moderate Terms
Stoke Poges (Sefton Arms)	"	9.54	3.14	5.8	6.44	—	—	3.16	4.56	6.44	
Gerrards Cross Station	"	10.10	3.28	5.24	6.58	9.30	—	3.30	5.10	6.58	
Chalfont St. Peter (The Church)	"	10.17	3.37	5.31	7.8	9.40	—	3.39	5.19	7.8	
Chalfont St. Giles (The Pheasant)	"	10.26	3.44	5.36	7.17	9.49	—	—	—	7.17	
Amersham (The Griffin Hotel)	"	10.39	3.53	5.45	*7.26	9.58	1.0	—	—	*7.26	
Oakfield Corner	"	10.52	4.2	5.57	7.32	—	1.9	—	—	7.32	
CHESHAM BROADWAY	arr.	11.2	4.15	6.10	7.42	—	1.20	—	—	7.42	

CHESHAM AND HIGH WYCOMBE.

		a.m.	p.m.			a.m.	p.m.	
CHESHAM BROADWAY	dep.	8.45	12.5	HIGH WYCOMBE (Top of Hill)	dep.	10.45	2.55	Through fare Chesham to H Wycombe 1s. 6d.
Amersham	"	9.10	12.25	Amersham	"	11.35	3.50	
HIGH WYCOMBE (Top of Hill)	arr.	10.0	1.20	CHESHAM BROADWAY	arr.	12.0	4.15	

S.O., denotes Saturdays Only. S.E., Saturdays Excepted. *Departs from Chequers. The Company give notice that they do not hold themselves responsible for any loss or inconvenience through failure to keep the printed service times consequent on breakdown or any other cause. Children over 3 and under 14 years of age, half fare.

Amersham & District Motor Bus and Haulage Co., Ltd.,
Griffin Garage, Amersham.

Advertisement placed by A&D in Bucks Examiner 22nd August 1922

In September, Mr Abrahams wrote in to see if he can fix adverts on the new bus. The Board concluded that because it is a small vehicle they would not allow advertisements on it for now.

By the end of September 1922 the National N6 route is further extended to finish in Berkhamsted. A&D had been given permission for this route in May 1921 and they had not taken it up. This must clearly be seen as an opportunity lost to the company.

The Company's financial year ended on 30th September and takings had barely increased year on year, rising to just £3183, the Board stated that it had been "a very wet summer". No dividend was able to be paid and the Directors had still not claimed a penny in expenses or salary; they were though upbeat about prospects and expected to be running three charabancs and two bus routes profitably the following year. The three charabancs would come about because of the up coming conversion of lorry BH8331 (see next photo). The minutes go on to show charabanc No 3 was insured the following May for the start of the next season. The Company never referred to more than three charabancs under their control at any one time. No mention of owning any lorries appeared after this time, so it is possible they quietly dropped that side of the business. Their full registered name, however, including the word "Haulage" remained unchanged.

Charabancs were very large vehicles weighing over 4 tons each, they returned between 10-12 mpg and were capable of 20 mph but officially restricted to 12 mph on solid tyres. Apparently they "shook themselves to bits over 20 mph" (quote from a driver of London Transport Museum's preserved 1914 Leyland). Customers certainly better appreciated models with pneumatic tyres, but no photographs of A&D charabancs thus fitted have been found.

In itself, Amersham was a destination for charabanc tours from London. On-board guides would stand facing the passengers, addressing them through loud hailer cones. Imagine an echo of information about 16th century coaching inns and martyrs burning at the stake rolling down the High Street in the wake of a charabanc dust cloud heading into the distance toward Great Missenden!

The public's love for the charabanc grew and grew, such that there was barely a square mile of England that one had not visited with its cargo of tourists. Some of the favoured destinations would seem quite strange to us now, this contemporary account was written by H.V. Morton whilst on a trip to Dartmoor; "All day long charabancs run into Princetown and pile up in the square. A morbid curiosity draws thousands of people to the melancholy Town of the Broad Arrow. Old women, small shopkeepers, young girls, troop down towards the nearest work-gang and stand, very solemn, and awed watching the men whom society has removed for its own safety. "Who's that, and what did he do?" is the question they all ask. The warders are not communicative. They stand at ease with their rifles, watching the men, seldom talking. What the convicts think as they see the herd of curious law-abiding folk gazing at them with a zoo expression is perhaps not at all printable." Extract from Morton's book "In Search of England".

Dennis charabanc BH8331 was registered by A&D in October 1921 as a green lorry. Not long after this date it was given this body which seems to sit awkwardly high off the ground, even for those days. It may be that this body was a second-hand one that is recorded in the minutes as being bought in November 1922 for just £35. A strange condition was attached to that purchase, in that it was not to be named "Somme". In the photo BH8331 has the number 3 on its bonnet. The charabanc behind is the older BH0348 and the different liveried Leyland bringing up the rear (AR 9424) may have been on hire to A&D. Photograph taken on The Broadway, Old Amersham.
Photo W Randall collection

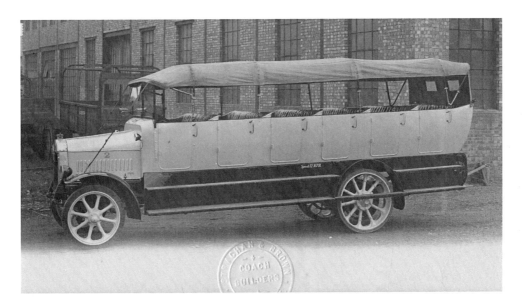

Dennis charabanc A&D bonnet no. 2, seen here at Strachan and Brown body builders, Acton, London, note speed restriction lettering limiting to 12 mph. This is almost certainly the same chassis as shown outside the Kings Arms Amersham in the previous chapter. This picture may have been taken following a body refurbishment exercise. The front bulk head (scuttle) is different; probably a weak point being made stronger, the lighting has been upgraded and grab handles added to aid climbing aboard. On close inspection the hood and seats do not look new. Photo W Randall collection

A later rear view of P3569 Dennis charabanc no. 2, just visible is "THE PRIDE OF BUCKS" logo.
Photo W Randall collection

A&D did not always have weighty things to worry about, recorded in the closing months of 1922 the Company received a claim from a Mrs Walton for damage to her dress caused by the bus body, this is settled fairly quickly with a payment of 7/6. The Company also started selling the advertising rights on their tickets to Brandons furniture store in Chesham. Brandon and Sons stores on Chesham Broadway can be seen behind the bus and on the right in the postcard image earlier in this chapter.

A COMPANY ON THE MOVE

At the board meeting on 22nd November 1922 it was recorded that the Chairman, Mr Charles Ivins and Mr Will Randall (Manager) owned land called Dovecot Meadow, on The Broadway, virtually opposite The Griffin and on it they proposed to finance the erection of a garage and offer the plot to the A&D Board at £160 per annum rent. Before the year ended this was all agreed with the Board and the Company was set to move across the road and away from Mr Miles rather cramped garage.

Dovecot Meadow is the walled field containing a horse shown on the left of this photograph. The buildings on the right are still readily identifiable today, being at the east end of town.
Photograph courtesy of Amersham Museum.

Hoping for improved fortunes, the Company looked forward to 1923, their fifth year of operation. By April they had transferred operations to their new site on The Broadway. The garage of the expanded premises was built of wood and corrugated iron and covered about 400 sq. yds. It could potentially accommodate about a dozen single deck buses. The move meant that the company could sell petrol from their own pumps and have enough garage space to perform motor vehicle repairs and offer storage, all of which would provide valuable additional revenue streams. The new roadside frontage afforded far easier off-road parking and space for manoeuvring vehicles. A separate existing small building acted as a headquarters and staff room.

Drawing N Lamond after Patterson

This year the company's Chesham to Slough route was extended to terminate and turn round at Windsor. Two later handed-down accounts give us some extra insight into those days nearly 100 years ago. The first is that the original Windsor service terminated by a field adjacent to the King Edward VII hospital. For quite a few years the only occupant of the field was a donkey who ambled over to meet every bus in the hope the conductor had a tasty morsel for him, which he usually did! The second tells us that the Windsor buses crossed at the Sefton Arms Hotel, Stoke Poges and this hostelry often became the venue for an unofficial break in the journey. The conductors would ask if anyone was in a hurry and this would be the cue for passengers to disembark into the pub for a pint and the crews to enjoy a quick game of darts!

It is in 1923 that the company also planned a third route, this time from Amersham to Beaconsfield via Holmer Green and Chalfont St Giles, another 14-seater bus was ordered in May. A new Crossley was chosen costing £482, also that month Charabanc no. 3 came on stream and was insured.

Their annual report in September was the first upbeat one since 1920. Takings had actually leapt by 50%; they now had three buses running regular routes. The Syndicate had been fully re-imbursed; the Company had also paid for the 1922 Oldsmobile (No 1) bonnet number 4 and almost fully paid for the new Crossley. The Company paid £440 for the Oldsmobile and reported buying yet another old charabanc body for £40. The Directors recorded that they will be discussing the possibility of a shareholder dividend for the first time. This expansion came at a time when they placed no local paper advertising for the entire year. In October Brandons were given permission to fix advertising boards to both sides of the Oldsmobile.

Years later the staff gave a huge amount of credit to their manager, Will Randall for the company's improving fortunes. It was often said how important he took feedback from staff and customers when things had gone wrong or improvements were suggested. Apparently, he asked conductors always to report when their bus was full and potential passengers were left waiting for the next one. He sometimes asked a senior driver to take out a spare bus or go and oversee events. Mr Randall also often travelled out in the company car to see first hand how operations were running.

The Directors must have had great impetus for 1924 given the wonderful results recently announced at their AGM. In January they ordered a new Dennis chassis and commissioned Strachan and Brown of North Acton to build a 14-seater body for it. By February it seemed Dennis Bros. had reported delays in the chassis build and the Directors removed the order from them and bought another Oldsmobile chassis for £252, this was delivered to Strachans and finished later that month, for a total cost of £417. Also purchased in February 1924 was an inexpensive second-hand 20 hp GMC station bus for £185.

The new 1924 Oldsmobile is photographed by Strachan & Brown after they supplied and fitted the body. The registration (not entirely clear above the windscreen) is PP1344, it was given bonnet no. 7. Note the new A&D monogram and the further reduction of the Company name, now also omitting "& District". The livery includes white upper parts, a theme to be continued. Photograph W Randall collection.

A little 14-seater bus as pretty as this new Oldsmobile, must have put a smile on the faces of locals as she chugged along the verdant Chiltern lanes. Blending in with the countryside but also standing out as a wonderfully liberating new service to a raft of small communities along her route. However it seems trouble was never far away for the Company and the old AEC bus now needed some much bigger repairs to its ageing body. Its solid tyres and the miles of roughly-made road surfaces meant the vehicles effectively shook themselves so much the wooden jointed framework sagged and separated. Even so, it was still a big earner for the company as the takings figures for the four weeks to 2nd March 1924 show:-

AEC	£61/14/4
Olds No 1	£82/7/10
Olds No 2	£17/0/5
Crossley	£58/5/9
Chara No 1	£15/9/6
GMC	£19/6/7
Chara No 3	£21/14/-

Note: The numbers in the list e.g. "Olds No 1" are those as recorded in the minutes and do not refer to their issued bonnet numbers, although this may not be the same for the charabancs. Charabanc No 2 was perhaps off the road at the time of this report as its figures return in the one given to the Board on 14th May.

The overall takings for 1924 show another good improvement, rising from £4821 at 30th Sept 1923 to £5963 a year later, all seemed to be going well and the investment was finally paying off. Also recorded in the accounts was the appointment of Dr. H J Henderson to the Board of Directors.

The following year saw further expansion for A&D with the purchase of two new Dennis buses; these were single-deckers with Strachan and Brown bodies. The first was to be delivered in March and the next illustration seems to be an original Strachan and Brown drawing for the proposed bus. However, the drawing and the photograph that follows it, appear to be so identical, even the wheels are stopped in the same position, that it may actually be an engraving from the photo. The company may have required a line drawing for advertising purposes; reproduction of photographs was still difficult in some printing processes. The bus is shown with solid tyres and displays bonnet number 9, it cost A&D £1123. Solid tyres were still being fitted to heavier type vehicles in 1925.

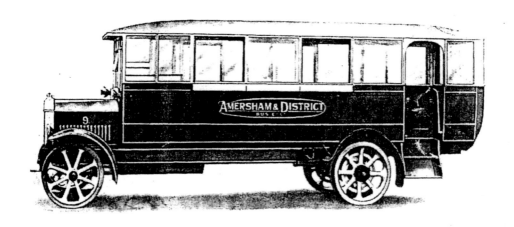

Dennis 3.4 ton 30/32-seat, registered March 1925, A&D bonnet no. 9, PP3477.
Photograph W.Randall collection.

The above drawing is possibly the first time the Company's next logo went on show, but it seems it wasn't their own flair for design that had created it. In 1923 a Hickman bodied double-decker Dennis bus (PD8344) was displayed at the Commercial Motor Show at Olympia in Aldershot & District livery. The vehicle sported a new Aldershot & District logo, an elongated loop oval framing their name in exactly the same style as we now see from Amersham & District. So, it seems that Aldershot & District got there first and Amersham copied them, possibly with the help of Strachan & Brown who, after 1923 had become Aldershot & District's body supplier of choice. No complaint from Aldershot & District is recorded in Amersham's minutes but it might also be questioned if they themselves had in turn taken the idea from Arnold & Comben coachbuilders of Farnham who had already established a very similar logo.

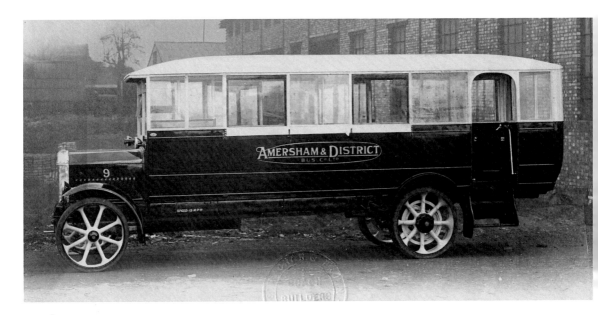

From the previous illustration to the finished article. The brand new A&D no. 9 is photographed as it came out of the build shop at Strachan & Brown. On the reverse of this original photo "3.4 ton" is written in pencil.
Photograph W Randall collection.

An early A&D bus makes its way out of Chesham. The photo dates from C1926 and the vehicle is probably either the company's GMC or Crossley vehicle.
Photo John Hutichinson collection.

Dennis 2.5 ton, 15 foot wheelbase model, registered PP4089 in May 1925, A&D bonnet no. 10. Keen eyes will notice the misspelling "The Chalfants" on the slip board of this freshly liveried bus.
Photo J Hutchinson collection.

A further similar, but lighter, Dennis was delivered in May 1925 and given bonnet no. 10, it is recorded the Company paid £1100 for this bus. As the photo shows the bus on pneumatic tyres but later minutes appear to record the first larger bus with pneumatic tyres that was acquired by the company did not arrive until November 1926, it therefore suggests that this photo, which shows a pristine no. 10, was taken after a subsequent refit. In the photo it is also displaying "trade plates" with the number 041BH. Smaller buses with around 14 seats had been fitted with pneumatic tyres for many years at this stage.

It was in 1925 that London saw the arrival of its first double-deck buses with roofs; unbelievably they had previously been banned by the police as it was felt they may make buses top heavy. Pneumatic tyres also started to appear on the heavier buses; again something the police had previously thought would be dangerous to permit.

The extra new bigger Dennis vehicles released the smaller Oldsmobiles to run a new route that opened on 4th May 1925, a service from Chesham Moor – Chartridge – Lee Common – Ballinger – Gt. Missenden running 5 times daily was advertised in the Bucks Examiner. This is still a truly pretty route on which to travel.

This photograph is of the 1922 Oldsmobile A&D bonnet no. 4, probably taken shortly after the start of the Chesham to Great Missenden route. A very young looking driver named Jim Chapman poses by his vehicle and he actually joined A&D on 25th May 1925 with the purpose of driving 14-seaters.
Photo Jim Chapman collection

THE AMERSHAM & DISTRICT MOTOR BUS & HAULAGE CO., LTD.

ADDITIONAL SERVICE COMMENCING 4th MAY, 1925.

Chesham to Great Missenden.

Announcement in the press May 1925

This is a photo of Oldsmobile A&D bonnet no.7 in use on the Chesham Moor to Great Missenden route via Ballinger, Lee Common and Chartridge. The sign in the side window is promoting a "GRAND FETE" on Saturday September 6th or 16th. Driver Jim Chapman looking very proud. Photo Jim Chapman collection.

William James Chapman (Jim) was born in Chalfont St Giles; after school he worked in a cycle shop and on leaving education he worked for aircraft firm AVRO's, then moving on to do some chauffeuring. In 1925 Jim's friend S Marchant (Bob) who already worked for A&D put in a good word about him to Will Randall. Mr Randall wrote and offered him a job as a 14-seater bus driver, as long as he could demonstrate a reasonable competence "to do ordinary roadside repairs" to vehicles. He would pay him £3/-/- per week for the first twelve months and then £3/5/-.

On 11th August 1925 an article was written about A&D in a weekly publication called "Commercial Motor". The column examines how small passenger carriers had developed in recent years and some had become flourishing concerns, it marks out A&D as amongst the better run who were succeeding against formidable difficulties. Success was coming from the initiative and enterprise of the directors. The article mentioned the two original 26-seater Scouts and the AEC lorry along with their first route between Amersham, Chesham and High Wycombe. The service was of particular value in so far as no means of transport otherwise existed for connecting with the lines of the Metropolitan and Great Western Railway Companies. Their "Pride of Bucks" motor coaches were also mentioned for their reliability and comfortable bodies, becoming highly recommended and patronised. It listed the 1925 fleet as "three Dennis 28-seater coaches, two 32-seater Saloon buses of the same make (the bodies of which were built by Messrs. Strachan and Brown), a 26-seater saloon bus, two 14-seater Oldsmobiles, one 14-seater Crossley and one 14-seater G.M.C. The Company expressed "particular satisfaction with the Oldsmobiles, bearing in mind the work they performed. The first machine of this make, bought in 1922, covered an average of 106 miles per day for 12 months without a mechanical breakdown." The Company further said "credit must also be given to the drivers, as there is little question that a big percentage of the life of any vehicle is due to the careful driving and attention which it receives". The article was illustrated using the images shown in this chapter of their Oldsmobile bonnet no. 7 and the recent purchase, the much larger Dennis 3.4 ton bonnet no. 9. We will see no. 9 a few more times as the Company's story progresses.

The A&D Board also ordered a third 26-seater from Strachan & Brown in late November, but this was not delivered until the New Year. One interesting move the directors made was to buy a second-hand Oldsmobile lorry from H Lewis of Chesham for £32, they then swapped the GMC bus body on to that Oldsmobile chassis and put the lorry bed onto the GMC. This made the Oldsmobile bus ready for service in 1926 and the GMC lorry was put up for sale. Presumably reliability and some fleet standardisation would have been at the centre of this idea.

It would seem that up until now timetables must have been posted as handbills on local walls etc. as in September 1925 the Board sanctioned the making of some frames in which to house and protect timetables around their area.

Later this year A&D extended the three routes currently terminating in Chesham to run on to the village of Ley Hill. Here they were able to use the Common and the service road in front of the pubs as a turn around facility. This book's cover illustrates an early vehicle dropping off passengers by the golf course. The extended services were appreciated by the residents along the route but in November some actually moaned to the local press that more could be done to help people arriving at Chesham Station on later trains.

EXPANSION PAYS DIVIDENDS

At the end of 1925 the Directors proudly announced a shareholder's dividend of 10%, up from 5% the previous year. They had now completed two good years of growth after 6.5 years of trading. Expansion and some vehicle replacement could now be confidently planned and the Company went on something of a spending spree in 1926.

The new 26-seater Dennis bus ordered before Christmas was delivered in January and given bonnet No. 11. At this time the directors took, the probably sad decision, to dispose of the AEC bus, their first vehicle and a reliable bus that became the bedrock from which they had grown the business. They now had eight buses and were working four main routes with numerous short runs between Chesham and Amersham. With the departure of the AEC (sold to Mr E Salter in Slough for £145) another new Dennis 2.5 ton 26-seater was ordered from Strachan and Brown at a cost of £1035 and was in use by March, this being given the bonnet no. 12.

For the 1926 Easter weekend A&D ran special return services to Windsor. This advert from the Bucks Examiner of 2nd April 1926 was the only advert A&D placed in this local paper throughout that year.
Advert reproduced from the Bucks Examiner April 1926

The reverse of a bus ticket showing one way of self promoting the Company.
Image courtesy of The Omnibus Society and dates from the early 1930's

Easter is clearly a time that people wanted to get out and about. This Bank Holiday spawned a super letter that appeared in the local press on 25th April 1926 giving us a wonderful insight into how the new mobility played out in the Chiltern area. The following transcription is exactly as printed.

THE MOTOR-WAY

Capitalists (blessed word!) are credited with the intention of running a motor-way through this district, and people have fears of a night and day whizz and whirl. But if and when the motor-way fructifies shall we have more motors through this and adjacent districts than we had this Eastertide? The general opinion seems to be that Chesham was full as usual, for the holidays; but no more full than usual. But inquire where you will upon the main roads and the story is the same – a Record Number of Motors. The rigours of Winter kept a good many of the motors in cold storage; the sunshine of Easter brought them out. Seated within view of a roadway which crosses one of our famous commons on Saturday, I was in conversation with an inhabitant about the traffic through that district upon the preceding day (Good Friday) and he expressed the opinion that they had never before known such a quantity of traffic in one day – the stream of motors seemed never ending and never pausing, and never lessening. As a curiosity we timed the motors for a quarter-of-an-hour and 30 passed – 120 an hour, and that, my friend was of opinion, a flea bite to the previous day. The variety and condition of motors out is amazing and four features struck you wherever you were (1) the number of ladies driving cars – some their husbands and some their own (in two or three cases on Saturday afternoon I saw motor parties with ladies in one car and gentlemen in another and in one case was asked by a lady driver the best place to stop for tea, and when directions were given the driver of the gentlemen's car sang out to the leading lady "Right ho! Old bean! You're leading this expedition, we'll "grub" where you do!" (2) the family parties in quite small cars or accommodated in many ways in side car and upon motorcycle; (3) the parties which were carrying their own luncheon baskets and catering for themselves (with the aid, of course, of the firm who pack these dainty luncheon baskets) and (4) the number of motor campers this early. If a lot of motorists catered for themselves, a large number patronised the restaurants, and speaking to one proprietor whose premises are upon a busy road, and asking him if he was busy on the previous day, his reply was "Goodness - don't speak about it we were run off our legs and one of my girls has not turned up to-day!" One of the funniest experiences I had – it had a funny side –was the finding of a motor party quite still in a busy road which runs parallel with a wood. It was not a desirable place to pause, in some ways, and I thought they had either had a breakdown or had missed their way. Enquiring the why and wherefore, I was told "No it's all right old-man, we're listening to the cuckoo!" And sure enough in the depths of the wood the blithe bird could be heard heralding the sunshine and bidding defiance to winter's terrors. "That's fine" said one enthusiast, "I've heard it several mornings recently" I replied. And the enthusiast laughed and said, "H'm I've heard the early morning tramcars - that's my early morning cuckoo call!"

The new freedom of movement was not restricted to the lucky few with their own motor cars; the buses running throughout the weekend brought in people from the bigger towns on the outskirts of London or directly from the train stations. These rising numbers greatly added to the newly found profitability of the Company.

At the end of September 1926 Messrs C. Ivins and W. Randall offer to sell to the Company the garage they currently rent to them, along with two adjacent bungalows to the east. The asking price was £3000 for the plot and buildings.

In the minutes for November it was recorded that Mr Randall had been to Guildford (the home of Dennis Bros.) and ordered a further new 30-seater bus, this time with pneumatic tyres and electric lighting (inferring it was a first). The electric lighting referred to maybe interior lights. Earlier photographs reveal that electric lighting was already in use for exterior lights and pneumatic tyres were standard fitment to lighter vehicles. So this bus was the first in the heavier category to have pneumatic tyres. It was delivered on 23rd November 1926 and cost £1115. Bucks CC licensing records show on 13th November 1926 this new Dennis coach was issued with the registration PP7144, the annual tax on it to be £60.

PP7144 was allocated bonnet no. 6, a 1926 Dennis 2.5 ton chassis with typical Strachan and Brown bodywork. The photo illustrates that at least 4 of the 5 offside windows open fully, wonderful for a summer's day in The Chilterns. Photo W Randall collection.

Guaranteed to confuse later historians, A&D adopted a method of re-using old bonnet numbers and, although not recorded in their minutes it is likely that the GMC bus had originally been number 6. (the GMC had been disposed of earlier in the year).

Another chance to see Dennis PP3477 A&D bonnet no. 9. This time making her way gracefully on a very peaceful stretch of road between Chesham and Amersham on route to Windsor. On the back of this photo is written "The "old" New Road, Chesham", it is now called Amersham Road but was called "New Road" when the original cart track was updated in 1820. No. 9 is still running on solid tyres at this time. Photo John Hutchinson collection, original taken by Fulton Bros. Amersham for the A&D Company.

The Bucks C.C. archived licensing records from this period show two levels of annual tax (presumably Road Tax and separate from an operating licence) £60 for larger buses and coaches and £30 for smaller 14-seat type vehicles. The fleet was really building now with the buses becoming more modern. Solid tyres were still in use on the older heavier vehicles right into the 1930's but some were converted to use pneumatics.

In December 1926 the Company paid Marlborough Motors (a St. Albans based dealer) £600 for a new chassis (almost certainly a Lancia that we will see in Chapter 7) and subsequently Strachan and Brown £405 for its new body. The two combining to form a new bus that was a probable replacement for their first Oldsmobile (bonnet no. 4 of 1922 and the new Lancia was given the same number), there is a record for selling this and Charabanc no. 3 in the accounts to 30th September 1927. Finally as the year came to a close one of the Company's founding directors Mr A C Norman died.

This photograph and the one that follows show lovely period street scenes from Amersham and Chesham. In the photo above we see A&D Dennis PP7251 (delivered new in December 1926) and re-using bonnet no. 3, its destination is set for Chesham during the annual Amersham summer fair. How lovely to see the traction engine in full steam, just resting between jobs.
Photograph courtesy of Amersham Museum

This photograph of Chesham Broadway c1926 shows how buses and traffic were starting to affect day to day life in the town. The two open topped double-deck buses are running on the National N6 route from Watford to Berkhamsted. The small A&D bus in the middle of the photo is PP1344 Oldsmobile bonnet no.7 and the A&D bus on the right hand side is a larger Dennis vehicle.

Photograph R East collection courtesy of Peter Hawkes.

The 1926 built Dennis 2.5 ton PP7251 bonnet no. 3 is shown here waiting on the stand at The Fountain, Frogmore, High Wycombe with the word "RELIEF" in the later fitted destination box.

Photograph taken in May 1933 by J F Higham, image courtesy of A B Cross collection.

A smaller Dennis 30 cwt. 14-seater, PP7700 with A&D bonnet no. 14 is photographed new in March 1927. Unusually for Strachan and Brown the door does seem a little out of place on an otherwise well sculpted body.
Photo W Randall collection.

The small Dennis 14-seater, PP7700 was the only vehicle ordered by A&D in 1927. Once again the Dennis chassis had been delivered to Strachan and Brown for a body to be fitted. This small bus was set to operate the Chesham to Great Missenden route and Strachan & Brown had its destination boards all prepared ready in the photograph taken outside their factory in Acton, North London.

The last main advertisement that has come to light for charabanc tours appeared on 22 July 1927 and is shown overleaf. However, A&D were still promoting charabanc hire as late as 1931 in their timetable booklets.

This advert appeared for A&D in the Bucks Examiner during July 1927 promoting their mid-summer charabanc tours. The prices seem quite high as a percentage of average wages, so this was certainly a treat if it could be afforded.
Advert reproduced from the Bucks Examiner July 1927

When we consider that solid tyred vehicles like the Company's charabancs were legally restricted to 12 mph, a journey to the south coast would have been a huge undertaking. Following a 6:30 am start, it must be expected the trip took 5-6 hours. Aiming to arrive at lunchtime and probably setting off for home at 4:00 pm to get back for 10:00 pm.

The Directors did record one complaint in their August minutes. It was from Mr G Shilton of Clifton Road, Chesham who pointed to overcrowding on the Chesham to Amersham bus and rudeness of conductor Brown on the 2nd of that month.

The A&D accounts for 1927 revealed they spent a total of £2794 on vehicles this financial year.

Fifteen months had now passed since the Directors were first offered the bungalows and land for sale and in January 1928 they made an offer of £2000 which was rapidly rejected. In February they finally agreed the original asking price of £3000.

The old Crossley was now put up for sale, but with seemingly no takers the Company went ahead and obtained a quote on a 14-seater Chevrolet. The Crossley was eventually traded-in for £70 with Marlborough Motors (St. Albans) against the Chevrolet which cost £400. The order however, is unexpectedly delayed and not completed until December that year.
The Company also gave Dennis Bros. an order for a coach chassis (Dennis F model) costing £885 (less 10% discount) and had a lovely 30-seater body made for it by Strachan & Brown for £475.

Above we see the Dennis F coach, A&D bonnet no. 15, bought early in 1928, until this photo came to light no existing record had been found that the vehicle was a soft top all-weather convertible model. This was the first of a number of coaches bought to satisfy the tour operation business with the added flexibility of performing bus work if required. Jim Chapman, the driver that day, enjoys a cigarette. The bows tied to the radiator may signify he is hired for a wedding party trip.
Photo Jim Chapman collection.

The A&D charabancs must surely have been used less and less from 1928 when they purchased this stunning looking Dennis coach with all-weather convertible bodywork (KX470). This year the company also tried to sell Charabanc no. 2; it is unclear from the minutes if this was finally successful, but amazingly they then buy Fosters old charabanc for £160 (see photograph page 16, Chapter 2). Charabanc no. 2 probably had the greatest value at this time. Whatever the reasoning behind that move we may never know but it does seem clear that this type of vehicle is nearing the end of its life. All had solid tyres, which were now rapidly becoming a thing of the past and probably uneconomical to convert to pneumatics.

In order for the public to know the main points along a route, "slip boards" are often inserted in brackets on the sides of the vehicles. Final destinations were always shown on the front of the bus. Photo John Hutchinson collection.

Time to catch up with an old friend, here is Dennis bonnet no. 9 (the number can be seen on the bonnet in the original photograph) out earning its living, picking up on Chesham Broadway for the short run through Botley and on to Whelpley Hill. This is one vehicle that has now been converted to run on pneumatic tyres. We will meet up again with her in a later chapter.
Photo taken by J F Higham, courtesy of the A B Cross collection.

In February 1928 Chesham Town Council decided to stop allowing buses to park in The Broadway, instead asking them to move down and wait in Broad Street. This undoubtedly angered many people who needed to carry goods and parcels to the buses and a number of letters appeared in the press from disgruntled passengers. How long it took the council to rescind this order is not known, but rescind it they did.

The Company minutes reveal a further, but all new style of Dennis was ordered this financial year at a cost of £1389, the price indicates this was the Dennis E model that became bonnet no. 16 in March 1928.

Unlike the earlier photograph where the driver is in the Company's summer uniform, here is conductor Percy Hounslow and driver George. Percy modelling the Company's monogrammed heavy winter coat, in front of new Dennis E (PP9954 bonnet no. 16) waiting on Chesham Broadway, this photo is dated 1928. We catch a glimpse here of a new type of bus design with the driver sitting alongside the engine; this will remain the shape and style of buses for many years to come.
Photograph P Hounslow family collection.

Amersham and District Bus Coy., Ltd.

Week Days.							BUSES LEAVE CHESHAM FOR WINDSOR—							Sundays.
a.m	a.m.	a.m	p.m.	p.m.	p.m.	p.m.	p.m.	p.m.	p.m.	p.m.	p.m.	p.m.	p.m
7.45	9.20	11.20	1.20	3.20	5.20	7.20	12.50	1.50	2.50	3.50	4.50	5.50	6.50

BUSES LEAVE CHESHAM FOR HIGH WYCOMBE—

| a.m | p.m. | p.m. | p.m. | | | | p.m. | p.m. | | p.m. |
| 8.45 | 1.0 | 5.10 | 7.55S.O. | | | | Sundays— 1.0 | 3.20 | | 7.5 |

BUSES LEAVE CHESHAM FOR TRING—

Daily except Mondays.

| a.m. | a.m. | p.m. | p.m. | p.m. | | | p.m. | p.m. | p.m. | p.m. |
| 8.50 | 11.15 | 2.20 | 5.10 | 8.0S.O. | | | Sundays—2.0 | 4.15 | 6.45 | 8.45 |

BUSES LEAVE CHESHAM FOR AYLESBURY—

| p.m. | p.m. | p.m. | | | p.m. | p.m. | p.m. |
| 2.20 | 5.25 | 7.5S.O. | | | Sundays—1.30 | 4.35 | 7.25 |

S.O.—Saturdays Only.

BUSES FOR WINDSOR, HIGH WYCOMBE AND AYLESBURY, Depart from OAKFIELD CORNER, 12 minutes later. From AMERSHAM, 20 minutes later.

On 25th May 1928 this advert appeared in the Bucks Examiner and shows the main Chesham departures of buses to their most significant destinations.
Advert reproduced from the Bucks Examiner May 1928

In May the Board were told of an incident in Berkhamsted where a bus had injured a heifer. As there had been no record so far of A&D running services to Berkhamsted, we must assume this was one of their buses on private hire. Seemingly cattle markets still happened in the street in Berkhamsted at this time.

One really important event in the entire, but short, history of the Company started to unfold in June 1928 when the all powerful London General Omnibus Company (LGOC) wrote and asked to have a meeting with A&D management on 4th July. LGOC wanted to work with A&D on certain routes and a collaboration of that sort gave certain powers to the A&D Board, this proposal gained further momentum when Frank Pick of LGOC attended a further meeting on 4th September. Later in the year LGOC bought shares in A&D as the Board approved an increase in the nominal capital of the Company to £25,000 by the creation of new shares. This event would prove to be a massive boost in the fortunes of the Amersham & District Bus Co.

Amersham and District
Motor Bus and Haulage Company Limited.

August Bank Holiday Services
SUNDAY, AUGUST 5th. SUNDAY SERVICE.
MONDAY, AUGUST 6th. SATURDAY SERVICE. ALL ROUTES.

TRING SHOW.
THURSDAY, AUGUST 9th. FARE 1/1.
Buses will leave Chesham for Tring — a.m., 8.50. 9.30. 11.15. 11.45. p.m., 1.30. 2.20 5.10. 8.0.
Leave Tring for Chesham — a.m., 9.45. 12.20. p.m., 3.20. 5.30. 6.15. 7.0. 8.30. 8.45.

Advert reproduced from the Bucks Examiner August 1928

A&D were always thinking of ways to gain more passengers, so local events that might attract people to travel were seen as an opportunity to explore. The above advert placed on 3rd August 1928 is one such example, from it we can also see that the August Bank Holiday was at the beginning of the month in those days.

The Company didn't have any double-deck buses on its fleet at this time but the National Bus Company was still running older style open topped double-deckers on its N6 route from Watford to Berkhamsted. In August 1928 an unfortunate incident is recorded in the local press, National Bus Company conductor Mr Broadbent was on the top deck when passing under Blackhorse Bridge in Amersham; for years he had been warning passengers to keep their heads down but on this day forgot to heed his own instructions. His head hit the bridge and it is recorded he was conveyed to Watford War Memorial Hospital.

This new, extremely well appointed, Dennis 18-seater coach KX1326 is seen here, late in 1928, having been ordered in October and given A&D bonnet no. 13. Note the subtle, but important changes between 13 and (the year older) 14 on page 35.
Photo W Randall collection.

As 1928 drew to a close the Company managed to squeeze in yet another major purchase and a second Dennis E was delivered just before the New Year. This was registered KX1645 and given bonnet no. 18.

Although it does not seem to have been minuted by the A&D Board there appears to have been a change in the livery for some of the new vehicles purchased. Running alongside the Company's fleet in green and white some vehicles now sport a chocolate brown and cream paint job. A 1976 reference has been found written by John Parke, a youth often visiting his grandmother in South Buckinghamshire during the 1920's and he says "As mentioned already Penn had one E type but A&D had more and these were, I think, the first to sport the brown livery used in the company's later years although I never saw any of the normal-control Dennis buses in that livery". By normal control he means the driver was completely behind the engine as in no. 13 above.

1928 Dennis E, KX1645 A&D bonnet no. 18. A photograph taken at Gerrards Cross, here we can see the entirely new frontal design where the driver sits alongside the engine. Having brakes on all four wheels also made this a safer vehicle. A further eight of this model were ordered in 1929 as the A&D business expanded.
Photo taken by J F Higham in 1932, courtesy of the A B Cross collection.

One of the eight mentioned above was KX1927 Dennis E bonnet no. 25 built in 1929, seen here picking up passengers but awaiting a driver. Unusually some of the bodies fitted to this model had spats (covers) over the rear wheels. The font of the bonnet number seems to range in size over the years, from minute up to this.
Photo by the late D.W.K. Jones courtesy A.D.Packer.

TURBULENT TIMES

The first of two truly tragic events occurring during this period happened on Thursday 15th November 1928 when an A&D bus ran over and fatally injured 7 year old Charles Edward Reuben Dean. Charles had hitched a lift on a motorbike to go home from school for lunch. He knew the motorbike driver but seems to have misjudged traffic passing when he stepped off the bike. The A&D driver, Mr Albert Brown of High Street Amersham said he was travelling at 18 mph when the boy stepped out in front of him, he sounded his horn instantly and stopped the bus in its own length, but it was too late and the boy had been hit badly. The A&D bus was on route from Chesham to Windsor and was on the Stoke Road heading for Slough when the incident happened. A Great Western bus had been travelling 100 yards in front of him and the boy tried to run between the two. The A&D conductor, Thomas Henry Rolfe, 142 Whieldon Street, Amersham, said he saw what happened and that the little boy ran into the bus. The driver was found to be totally without blame whatsoever and whilst having no liability the company made a payment of £5/0/0 to Mr W R Dean (father). Mr W Randall (A&D manager) along with others were reported as "all condoling with the father and the 16 year old motorbike driver" following the inquest.

To add to the Company's woes, the very next month on 6th December 1928 a bus was destroyed by fire, the insurance company pay out was £297/10/-. From the size of the payout it seems most likely this was Oldsmobile bonnet no. 7 PP1344 that we had seen photographed new, earlier in the book.

Whilst going through this troublesome period Amersham and District's working relationship with LGOC went largely unrecorded in the minutes but the significance of it can be seen from early on. In January 1929 A&D paid LGOC £417 deposit on buses so far supplied, they also minuted that they were looking into acquiring their own garage accommodation at High Wycombe. A&D had already started to jointly run a local route with Thames Valley buses and had two new Dennis E buses out-stationed at that company's Wycombe Marsh garage. This co-operation had come about through LGOC's links with both companies. For A&D it didn't take long to find a site for their own new garage as by April that year they offered £2000 for a plot on the corner of Marlow Hill and Queen Alexandra Road.

Also in January complaints from the public were aired in the press about new bus regulations that had curtailed buses stopping in the Market Square, Chesham and that the replacement boarding points were in desperate need of shelters during inclement weather. The authorities had made the restrictions because more and more bus services were plying in the area and, according to the report, these even included buses from London. With the increased traffic, the police became more active in prosecuting speeding. The old speed limit for heavy solid tyred vehicles still applied at 12 mph although it seemed to be largely ignored with only the occasional fine being issued. However, in February the driver of a 4 ton lorry was fined £2 for such an offence on a local road. By June the full extent of the increased bus traffic becomes apparent when a survey reveals that between 140 and 150 buses from all competing companies were now running through Chesham daily! Complaints that some bus operators were totally ignoring timetables and that buses dangerously passed each other to be first at the next stop, forced action from the Council who decided, at tax-payers expense, to appoint a "Bus Inspector" at £1 per week for a trial reporting period of three months. In researching this book, Janet Cussans, granddaughter of Will Randall, said the family always called the operators not running to proper timetables "chaser buses". The Council threatened to revoke operating licences of any company who received bad reports from the inspector.

On June 7th at 9:15 pm Albert Brown was driving his bus down Station Road Amersham when he stopped abruptly as a car coming up was overtaking another vehicle and blocking Albert's side of the road. The car couldn't stop in time and hit the side of Albert's A&D bus. Once again Albert was found totally blameless as he had been in the previous case only months before, a relief to him we can be sure.

The LGOC acquired a greater stake in A&D and by August 1929 they had gained control of the company by purchasing newly issued ordinary and preference shares. The annual accounts report for 30th September tells us a bit more about the company's rapid expansion, increased fleet size and the progress of a second extension to the Amersham premises, with completion due by December. The High Wycombe plot of land offer had gone ahead and building there was also nearing completion. The value of motor vehicles at cost, with depreciation, now stood at £20,000 - up from £8000 the previous year. Out of ten new vehicles bought by A&D, with that huge injection of LGOC cash, eight were Dennis E models and two were Gilfords. It was probably the two Gilfords that stood out from the crowd as they were both stunningly bodied by Strachans. These lower chassis vehicles made them look surprising sleeker than the higher Dennis E models.

KX1923 Gilford 166OT A&D bonnet no. 17 a 32-seat vehicle new to the company in February 1929. Photographed in 1933 outside the Astoria cinema in Chesham Broadway.
Photo taken by J F Higham, courtesy of A B Cross collection.

KX2595 Gilford 166SD A&D bonnet no. 27 a 30-seater all-weather coach delivered in May 1929. Photographed outside the original 1923 A&D garages on Amersham Broadway.
Photo taken by J F Higham, courtesy of A B Cross collection.

Amersham, August 1929. Couple on motorbike taken to hospital following serious collision with A&D bus. **See crash details and alarming newspaper front page photograph opposite. But did the lawyer acting for A&D have access to the vital evidence that was contained in the yet to be published newspaper photograph?**
Drawing N Lamond

Photo taken by T.C.Proffitt that made the front page of the Bucks Examiner

A head-on collision between one of Amersham & District's new Dennis E vehicles (KX2794, bonnet no. 26) and a couple on a motorbike made a nasty sight on the front cover of the Bucks Examiner. The accident happened at Oakfield Corner crossroads, Amersham on Sunday 11th August 1929 at around 7:00 pm. The A&D bus was being driven by Charles E C Stanbury of Widmer End, it was travelling from Chesham on the Windsor route when the collision with the motorcyclist and passenger occurred. Fortunately both people on the motorcycle were thrown clear and the mangled bike became lodged firmly under the bus. Despite substantial damage to the bike, a watch on the handlebars was said to still be ticking merrily the next day. Both cyclists were taken to hospital and spent time recovering from leg injuries. A&D lodged a claim for £6/14/6 against the motorcyclist, who counter claimed £300. The case went to Marylebone County Court but the judge urged them to settle before trial. The Company offered £150 plus costs which was accepted. The incident and photograph were not published until this agreement was reached in November 1930. The newspaper report recorded the injured motor-cyclist as Arthur Hall of Willesdon and his "pillion rider" as Lena Durnford of Harlesdon. However, as is very clear from the published photograph there is no pillion (seat) for a passenger! Should the defence have been that the motorbike was not being driven in a safe manner from the outset?

Bus tragedy in Ley Hill – April 1930

"Innocent play that ended in dire tragedy," "unavoidable because the careful driver and conductor could not hope to cope with the incalculable child mind" reported The Bucks Examiner from the inquest.

45

Death of Harvey Joiner

On Wednesday 2nd April just after 6:00 pm a group of boys playing on Ley Hill Common saw the Amersham bus coming down The Green. The bus stopped to set down passengers before making its turn in front of the pubs and as it did so four boys jumped aboard for a free ride. Two boys Harvey Joiner (8) and William Hewitt (aged 11 of 63 Ley Hill) mounted at the front door and Lawrence Bruton (13) and George Day at the rear door. It seems Harvey was swinging on a handrail as the bus turned to face The Swan, in an instant Harvey fell or jumped from the platform, bounced on a bank and was thrown back under the twin rear wheels of the bus. The driver felt the bus go right over something and stopped when he heard shouting. Harvey was unable to get up but didn't seem visibly injured and he was talking, he was carried to his house at 68 Ley Hill. A doctor was called and he was taken by ambulance to Chesham Cottage Hospital, his condition deteriorated overnight and he sadly passed away the next morning. An inquest took place and was reported in the Bucks Examiner for Friday 11th April. The conductor said the boys had played this prank before and he was constantly telling them off about it. The driver was William James Chapman of Chalfont St. Giles and the conductor William Frederick Surridge of Amersham. Harvey was the son of Mr and Mrs Ernest Joiner. The inquest found that Harvey's death was accidental. The bus was reported as an Amersham & District heavy Gilford 32-seater, un-laden weight of 5 tons 5 cwt. Amersham & District only had one Gilford bus on its fleet that matched the twin-door description; registration KX3928, bought new from Gilford's just prior to this accident.

Family wreath placed on Harvey's grave – April 1930
Photographs courtesy of the Joiner family.

A&D POWERING AHEAD

On a very wet 14th January 1930 poor Ernest Gomm, A&D conductor from Chesham, was working the last bus out of Gerrards Cross back to Amersham when a crowd leaving a "talkie picture place" rushed his 32-seater to ensure getting home. Poor Ernest felt over-whelmed and ended up with 12 standing, which was against the law. A policeman pulled the bus over and Ernest ended up in court. He pleaded his case well, claiming intimidation and also that a policeman at the stop had even asked him to take a further stranded couple. He got off with a warning, but the Bench added that they would not show leniency for a repeat offence.

Ernest's experience of heavy passenger numbers travelling on the Windsor route will have contributed to the Board considering their first purchase of double-deck buses. However, this route passed under Amersham's restricted height "Black Horse bridge" and necessitated the use of two special AEC Regents with so called "low-bridge" bodies; they were delivered in April and May that year. The two buses even had different body manufacturers, possibly indicating they were a rushed order that couldn't be satisfied by one manufacturer. However, when delivered both vehicles looked almost identical. They seated 48 passengers (24 on each deck) and featured sunken walkways on both sides of the top deck, meaning passengers sitting underneath them had to mind their heads as they stood up! In between the walkways were benches each seating three passengers.

One of the AEC Regent double-deckers purchased in April 1930, bearing A&D bonnet no. 29. Seen here at the Saracen's Head, Beaconsfield. Photo J F Higham in the A B Cross collection.

The two photographs above show the upper and lower interior of KX4656. The small signs on the 3-seater benches upstairs say "Caution Low Roof," the dual side gangways allow the conductor to walk all round when collecting fares. Down below those sunken gangways also have major impact on headroom.
Photographs J C Gillham March 1953 courtesy of the A B Cross collection.

It was mentioned earlier that the Company had chosen a new chocolate brown livery for some of its new vehicles and an unsubstantiated reference has been seen that the two new double-deckers were maroon and cream. Can we possibly suppose that maroon and chocolate brown are not too far apart to have become confused in memories?

KX4337 Dennis EV 32-seater was actually delivered a month before the double-decker shown previously and was issued bonnet no. 28. Seen here outside the cinema on Chesham Broadway. The EV variant had a far more powerful 6 cylinder engine than the 4 cylinder Dennis E models.

Photo taken by J F Higham and courtesy of the A B Cross collection.

The new Amersham & District bus garage at High Wycombe.

Photo W Randall collection

Overall the 1930 accounts mainly reveal that the fabulous new High Wycombe garage is now fully built, and with the Amersham one soon to be extended, the Board states both will be "efficient and well equipped". The value of motor vehicles has risen to £22,485 this year; this is a surprisingly small increase given that their fleet list has gone up by 5 vehicles when the accounts were drawn up. These were the 2 x AEC double-deckers, 1 x Dennis EV and 2 x Gilford's. It must be presumed that by now A&D are using some form of lease finance to procure vehicles and their purchase value is not reflected in their motor vehicle assets on the balance sheet.

The design of the vehicle bodies ordered by the Board continues to modernise and this will be seen over in the coming chapters. They have moved from the original and fairly austere bodies, through to high luxury vehicles with deep padded seating, curtains and sunroofs. We can see that travelling with the company was meant to be an experience, the drivers and conductors are always uniformed, with distinct outfits for summer and winter. Back at the beginning when the drivers sat out in all weathers, the Company had provided huge thick coats, now although vehicles are still without heating, the winter garments are thicker to provide warmth. The smaller vehicles are already one man operated, with conductors only needed on the larger ones.

The body on one of the new Gilford vehicles purchased in 1930 is similar to that of KX2595 bonnet no. 27 seen in the previous chapter. The lovely 30-seater with convertible (all-weather) open top was clearly the height of luxury on a summer day but also practical in less clement conditions. The Gilford chassis were built in High Wycombe and then taken to Strachans (Acton) Ltd. for bespoke bodywork to be fitted (note: name changed from Strachan and Brown in 1929).

Gilford 1680T chassis with Strachans all-weather bodywork, built 1930, Registered KX4984 A&D bonnet no. 31.
Photo W Randall collection.

As if in a child's pop up cartoon book, this photo shows the same Gilford (KX4984) being put to fun use for a works outing. The coach only had 30 seats so presumably some in the photograph didn't make the trip. Driver Jim Chapman would have had to exercise control over the number of passengers sitting on laps and keep an eye on the beer crates up top!
Photo J Chapman collection.

In late October the Board agreed to buy two small Dennis GL bus chassis for £435 and £425 respectively.

One of the Dennis GL chassis purchased in October 1930 comes off the production line at Strachans of Acton with a lovely 18-seat, very luxurious body and interior. KX5967 was given bonnet no. 33. See interesting changes in design of the streamlined roof destination box on this one compared to no. 13 on page 40. Photo courtesy of The Omnibus Society

In December 1930 a statement in the House of Commons was issued saying that all smaller bus operators in the area surrounding London must co-operate in order to achieve co-ordination with the London Passenger Transport Board. This transition was now being handled by Sir William McLintock, it was the beginning of the Government's decision to place all Underground and bus services within an approximate 30 mile radius of London under one controlling body. The idea was to run an integrated transport network where buses and Underground trains worked in co-operation to meet the capital's transport needs.

As Christmas approached the A&D Board announced a staff bonus of £1 for over 5 years service; 10/- for 2-5 years and 5/- for under 2 years. The Manager's (W Randall) commission would be 5% of bus and charabanc takings above that of the 1927 financial year. Finally, the Board were proud that in the past year, two apprentice's had been indentured, they were Donald Sidney Thomas Edwards and Frederick John Kaley. A copy for the indenture of 15 year old Donald Edwards shows that he was taken on by A&D as an apprentice "Motor Mechanic"; he was sponsored by "Amersham United Charities (Tothill's Charity)". The Charity would supplement his earnings over a four year training program (£12 upon signing on 17th December 1930 and two payments of £9 on 30th September 1932 and the same date in 1934). A&D agreed to give him full training and pay wages as follows:- 14 shillings per week in the first year, 15 shillings for the second, 20 shillings for the third and 25 shillings for the forth. The indenture was signed by Donald and his father William in the presence of C Ivins and G Knowles (Directors) and Geo. Stone (Secretary) for A&D.

Some older vehicles are being moved on by the Company around this time. Records show that charabanc (BH 0348) was finally traded-in as part of a deal involving the rather unusual purchase of two second-hand Guy double-decker buses in January 1931. No photographs have come to light of these vehicles nor have details of the use to which they were put.

The Road Traffic Act 1930 had come into force on 1st January 1931 and speed limits for buses and coaches were increased to 30 mph. As large numbers of buses still ran with no speedometer, driver judgement would be crucial. Public Service Vehicle (PSV) licences costing one shilling were introduced in 1930 for both drivers and conductors, and driving tests for bus drivers came in as well but even now were at the discretion of the Traffic Commissioners. For driver licence purposes, buses with an un-laden weight exceeding 2.5 tons were classified as "Heavy Motor Cars" and drivers now had to be over 21. The Highway Code was also introduced in 1931 and cost one penny, it was in a very different format to the current one. It advised sounding your horn if you were over taking and advised horse drawn vehicle drivers to use their whip to point left or right to indicate turning. Mirrors, or their use, didn't even get a mention. Conductors now had to be at least 18 years old to get a licence. The licences were initially issued by local councils and Ernie Revel remembered this causing trouble, some councils (he particularly remembered Aylesbury) didn't recognise the licence of another council, forcing operators to buy additional licences if their staff travelled into adjacent territories. The next photograph is of Ernie's original "Chesham" issued badge and he recalled having to swap this for an Aylesbury one when he passed into the area under their jurisdiction. The coming of the PSV licence allows us to date some photographs either side of this 1930/31 period, whether a driver or conductor is shown wearing his PSV licence badge or not.

Early licence badge issued to A&D conductor Ernie Revel.

It was made unlawful for drivers to work a continuous period of more than 5.5 hours before having a break of at least half an hour, with not more than eleven hours to be worked in any period of twenty-four. The Act contained a lot more rules that benefited drivers and conductors alike and in order that they understood them, the Transport and General Workers Union issued a very useful 120-page hard-backed booklet detailing all the relevant clauses and driving regulations contained within the new Highway Code.

Getting your name in the local paper will always cause a stir with friends and family. This must have been the case for A&D driver Frank Beale and his conductor Arthur William Gretton, when on route from Beaconsfield to High Wycombe on a foggy Jan 6th 1931, whilst manoeuvring around a milk float they were in collision with a Chrysler car. The car driver was certain they were to blame, whilst Frank felt totally innocent. The case didn't get settled until it came to court 18 months later, the judge found neither party had done anything actually wrong and each should bear their own costs. Repairs to the bus cost £24/18/8.

Also in January 1931, A&D launched an hourly express coach service running from Chesham to London via Amersham and Uxbridge. It had been LGOC's intention to run this service under their Green Line branding but that request was turned down by the authorities in favour of a local company running the operation. LGOC's control over A&D put them in a favourable position and their application was duly accepted. At least three 1930 AEC Regal T-class single-deckers were immediately supplied to A&D by LGOC's Green Line and they could start the service. A further one was added in April and another before the end of the year. Green Line were to supply the vehicles, tyres, licences and all outgoings whilst A&D were to charge back to them all operational, garage and administration costs. Following some research done by Nicholas Salmon of Chesham Bois in the 1980's he claimed to know that these five AEC Regals were painted in a Chocolate and Cream livery whilst operating for Amersham & District.

THE AMERSHAM & DISTRICT MOTOR BUS & HAULAGE COMPANY, LTD.

Reg. Office: BROADWAY, AMERSHAM.   Phones: Amersham 31.   High Wycombe 31.

EXPRESS COACH SERVICE
CHESHAM, UXBRIDGE & LONDON
Commencing FRIDAY, 13th FEBRUARY.

CHESHAM BROADWAY	A.M. 7 20	P.M. 7 20		LONDON (Oxford Circus)	A.M. 9 5	P.M. 9 5		Booking Offices :
Oakfield Corner	7 27	7 27		Shepherds Bush	9 23	9 23		Mr. R. Wright, Chesham Broadway.
Amersham (A. & D. Garage)	7 30	7 30		Acton (Six Bells)	9 33	9 33		Tel. No. 52 Chesham.
Chalfont St. Giles (Pheasant)	7 38	7 38		Ealing B'dy	9 40	9 40		Bucks Insurance Bureau Ltd., Oakfield Corner
Chalfont St. Peter (Church)	7 43	7 43		Hanwell (Lloyds Bank)	9 43	9 43		Tel. No. 77 Amersham.
Gerrards Cross (Station)	7 49	7 49		Southall	9 46	9 46		
Denham (Cross Roads)	7 57	7 57		Hayes (P.O.)	9 52	9 52		A. & D. Office, The Broadway, Amersham
Uxbridge (Garretts)	8 2	8 2		Hillingdon	9 55	9 55		Tel. No. 36 Amersham.
Uxbridge (R.A.F. Depot)	8 4	8 4		Uxbridge (R.A.F. Depot)	10 1	10 1		Post Office, Chalfont St. Peter.
Hillingdon	8 10	8 10		Uxbridge (Garretts)	10 3	10 3		
Hayes (P.O.)	8 13	8 13		Denham (Cross Roads)	10 8	10 8		Garrett, Uxbridge. Tel. No. 642 Uxbridge.
Southall	8 17	8 17		Gerrards Cross (Station)	10 16	10 16		Orange Coaches, 6 Shepherds Bush Green.
Hanwell (Lloyds Bank)	8 22	8 22		Chalfont St. Peter (Church)	10 22	10 22		Tel. No. 2201 Reliance.
Ealing B'dy	8 25	8 25		Chalfont St. Giles (Pheasant)	10 27	10 27		The District Messenger Office, 279 Regent St.
Acton (Six Bells)	8 32	8 32		Amersham (A. & D. Garage)	10 35	10 35		
Shepherds Bush	8 42	8 42		Oakfield Corner	10 38	10 38		Southall Saloon Coach Booking Agency, 18,
LONDON (Oxford Circus)	9 0			CHESHAM BROADWAY	10 45	10 45		Broadway. Tel. No. 1409 Southall.

Sundays—First Coach leaves Chesham 9.20 a.m. and Oxford Circus 11.0 a.m. and then hourly until as weekdays.

This press advert from 15th February 1931 promotes the new A&D coach service which rapidly attracted a very large number of passengers. From the timetable we can see that the coach was only allowed a few minutes standing at Oxford Circus before needing to turn round and return. The photograph below illustrates what took place a few short months later.
Advert reproduced from the Bucks Examiner February 1931.

One of the AEC Regal T class coaches with Chiswick bodywork which transferred from Green Line to A&D in January 1931 in use on its London express coach route. This already carried London General bonnet no. T69 (reg. GF544) which it retained for duties with A&D. They say every picture tells a story and this one certainly does. The express coach route had originally started in Chesham with pick up points at Amersham, The Chalfonts, Gerrards Cross, Denham and Uxbridge. However, after a few months of operation, the South Eastern Traffic Commissioner did not allow the start at Chesham nor the stop at Denham. So the roof destination boards were hurriedly altered. On the top line of this coach the CHE of CHESHAM was painted out and AMER of AMERSHAM squeezed in and on the line below DENHAM was painted out completely. Photo by the late D.W.K. Jones courtesy A.D.Packer

54

Henry Gurney one of the original A&D directors passed away in March 1931. In April the company was offered a parcel of land amounting to 50 foot of extra frontage to their existing land on The Broadway, they agreed a purchase price with Mr William Green of £262/10/0.

In February and August 1931, A&D issued wallet sized timetable booklets describing all the routes currently operated by them. These aptly illustrate why they have been purchasing so many vehicles of late, they now run no less than 19 separate routes around the area. The timings of these routes indicate they required a minimum of 34 buses to operate them on a main stream day. From building up a fleet list (see page 87) of known vehicles at this time, we can see they would have had a small number extra to spare. This growth had influenced the A&D Board to commission the building of new offices, staff accommodation and waiting room at Amersham and these were ready for occupation in 1931.

Pricing for the express coach journeys initially fluctuated quite a lot, an October 1931 A&D timetable shows the return fare from Amersham to London as 3/- but it seems it increased considerably above that over the ensuing months. Express coach routes certainly became very popular and competition kicked in, such that price cutting then actually made some operations uneconomical. Within a couple of years the Metropolitan Traffic Commissioners stepped in and set a general rate for these journeys of 1d per mile single and ¾d per mile return. In the case of A&D at that time the ruling worked to their detriment, when they ended up with a full return cost at 3/3d, a reduction of 1s over their then former rate.

A luxury AEC Regal with dark green and cream bodywork by Strachans, bought in April 1931, this one registered KX6785 carried A&D bonnet no. 34. Seen here in Chesham having come down from Ley Hill on its way to Windsor. It went on to serve London Transport until 1953 as T364 (the roof rack was removed by LT and later still it was completely re-bodied). Photo J F Higham from the A B Cross collection.

By this time vehicles are being designed with more and more luxurious features. Specially appointed coaches capture greater grandeur on the longer trips. Smooth interior panelling, curtains, sunroofs, concealed lighting, interior mirrors, luxury seats and clocks in sunburst wood panelling echo the new art deco influences. A&D even adopt a new style of coach lining with fleurs-de-lis terminals to set off their paintwork. This all creates a way of life to which the new traveller could aspire, as ever it was enhanced by the immaculately turned-out driver and conductor teams who took such pride in these vehicles and their operation. Imagine what lovely summer countryside journeys could be had with the sunroof open and the windows down or even the hood fully back on the Company's all-weather coaches.

Photo J Hutchinson collection

The above photos show the final incarnation of the A&D garages and the brick built office block in Amersham. To the extreme left can be seen the earlier buildings and petrol pumps. These lower buildings were demolished in 1953 but the newer ones survived more than 60 additional years before making way for elderly living accommodation.
Photo courtesy Michael Rooum

When writing this book the oldest living residents could only remember A&D from their childhood days. In 2013 Margaret Long, a lifelong resident of Ley Hill village, recalled the A&D conductors asking some gentlemen to get off the bus if it couldn't cope with heavy passenger loads climbing Eskdale Avenue, Chesham. The men were requested to walk 100 yards or so to flatter ground before getting back on. A&D certainly still ran a number of older stock vehicles into the 1930's and these would struggle on the steeper Chiltern Hills. In 2016 Norman Freeman, a Chesham resident, recalled regularly seeing two or three A&D single-deckers parked overnight on the land, in Eskdale Avenue, alongside The Jolly Sportsman. These out-stationed vehicles would be the first daily ones used on Chesham departures and would be manned by Chesham based crews. Norman would later go on to have a career working on buses operating out of Amersham Garage.

SPECIAL BUS SERVICES TO THE DOGS' GARDEN PARTY IN BALLINGER!

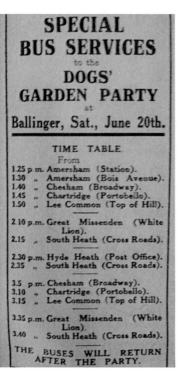

In the run up to 20th June 1931 this advert for a Dogs' Garden Party with an accompanying timetable for buses out and back to the event appeared in The Bucks Examiner. Life clearly proceeded unchanged in South Bucks despite the country facing the start of The Great Depression.

Advert as placed in Bucks Examiner

By September, Green Line decided that the charge back scheme for the loan of the London express coaches, arranged at the beginning of the year, is probably best replaced with a purchase scheme and A&D agree a repayment period over the next 8 years.

The value of Company vehicles increased to £26,214 when reported in the end of year, 30th September accounts. In October the board ordered another two AEC Regal vehicles and paid £1500 each for them including bodies from Strachans, see next photographs.

In October 1931 A&D purchased a further pair of AEC Regal coaches costing £1500 each. One of them shown here and again below is KX7634, given bonnet no. 36. The proud driver is Wilf Brackley pictured parked alongside a field in Windsor, this was destined to be site of the Windsor bus garage. The field was home to a donkey to whom the bus crews fed titbits. The destination is already set for its return to Ley Hill.
Photo J Hutchinson collection.

A second photograph of A&D bonnet no. 36, this time heading a line of buses waiting at The Fountain, Frogmore, High Wycombe.
Photos W Randall collection.

A&D ONLY AS GOOD AS ITS STAFF

One of the greatest pleasures in researching this book has been to unearth stories behind some of the Company's employees. It is the people that make a company what it is and it is their stories that are so often never recorded or told, so this chapter offers some small insight into a handful of those characters who are now departed and cannot speak for themselves.

William (Will) Randall played such an enormous part in building the Amersham and District Motor Bus Company business that it is appropriate to look at him first. He was born in 1892 and attended school in Penn Street, he then worked as a gardener at Woodrow House just a couple of miles from Old Amersham. At this time he gained invaluable driving and mechanical skills experience. It was here he met his future wife Kate, who was Lady's Companion at the house and they were married before the Great War. In late 1914 Will was called up for army service, joining up the following January. His driving skills saw that he was channelled into the RASCMT (Royal Army Service Corps Motor Transport) and he went straight to France. He was awarded the British War Medal and Victory Medal for his service.

On returning home after the war, he found work as a fitter at £3/15/0 a week with Mr E C Miles at The Griffin Garage, Amersham. As we have seen in other chapters, E C Miles was central to the start up of the bus operating business and after just 18 months trading Will was appointed the new bus company's Management Fitter. Now on £4/0/0 per week plus a bonus scheme of 5% of takings over £40. Clearly the bonus scheme was to ensure the buses ran as smoothly and reliably as possible. Years later Will's granddaughter Janet recalled how her grandmother said he always came home with clothes covered in oil and to get that off she soaked them in paraffin before washing them.

Within a short time Will was trusted by the Board to go to manufacturers, negotiate and order new buses. By the later 1920's he became the sole Manager of the entire business and his name appeared as such on the side of the vehicles along with the registered office details (see photographs of KX8643 bonnet no. 7 just behind front nearside wheel or Gilford no. 31). Every week the wages money was paid out to Will and then he distributed it to the staff. In 1932 he acted as co-negotiator in the takeover bid for Chesham and District Bus Co.

He often drank after work in the Iron Horse by Amersham Metropolitan station, discussing buses for hours at a time with some of the other directors.

He had close links and friendship with Charles Ivins, the Chairman, and spent some holidays with him. In 1930 they travelled to Paris and were photographed lounging in deckchairs on the Paris Plage. The following year they treated themselves to a First Class boat trip to Marseilles aboard the Dutch ship "Insulinde" bound for the Dutch East Indies. Will was 39 and Charles 54 at this time.

At the end of 1932 Will was awarded a manager's bonus of £593/5/3 and the directors set his salary for 1933 at a massive £720 per annum such was the regard they held for him. Will's story continues in Chapter 9.

A rather battered Randall family photograph showing Will (left) engaging in friendly banter with (probably) two of his drivers.

Gaining employment with the Company was eagerly sought as the roles were held in high regard by the community. The Company had a good reputation and staff turnover was low. The Company would go on to employ in excess of 100 people. It seems that one of the perks of the job was free travel on the Company's routes. The pass below was issued to Don Edwards.

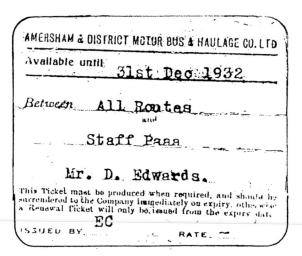

Every now and again photographs turn up with interesting side stories and the selection that follows provides a wonderful insight into a number of the staff.

In an earlier chapter there was reference to stopovers at The Sefton Arms on the Windsor route and below is a similar account from 1927 which also refers to a pub break!

The album caption under this photo states "Jack and me at the Fox and Pheasant, Stoke Common, 1927. Bus no. 4." Jack is the driver (on the left) and the conductor is Percy Hounslow. This photo also shows the Lancia ordered by the Company in late 1926 to replace the original Oldsmobile no. 4 and in turn re-used that bonnet number.
Photo 1927 Mr Hounslow collection, courtesy of The Amersham Museum.

Percy Hounslow was born in 1909 and lived in the hamlet of Woodrow, near Amersham. He joined A&D when he was 14 and claimed he was their youngest ever conductor. He rode a bicycle to the garage each day. He mainly worked on routes listed as 1 and 5 in Appendix 2. Percy met a young lady who, every Friday, caught the A&D bus from the top of Amersham Hill in High Wycombe and travelled to Amersham, changing on to the A&D bus for Aylesbury where she lived. On Mondays her journey was reversed as she worked the week in service in High Wycombe. This friendship turned to romance and the couple married in 1930, they made their home in Hazlemere.

The drivers and conductors work was not necessarily over the instant they returned the bus to the garage. If it was also the end the day, the vehicle had to be filled with petrol and, as Percy Hounslow often told his son, the conductor had to sweep out the vehicle as well as completing his "day sheet" thus logging his ticket sales and running times. The dusty and mud splattered vehicles were then handed to the cleaning and maintenance staff. They underwent a washing process involving hand spraying and long handled brushing to remove every speck of dirt and grim. They were hand dried off and given a buff over. Meanwhile mechanics would give the chassis and running gear a quick look over. Once a week the buses would go over the pit, brakes adjusted, tyres de-flinted and faults tracked down. The maintenance staff could work well into the early hours to have the whole fleet ready for an early start in the morning.

Driver Wilf Brackley was just coming to the end of his run from Ley Hill to Coleshill Church when to his surprise the road ahead of him was blocked by a wheel barrow. He stopped the bus and got down to move the offending object when someone snapped him in the act. He was later given a copy of the photograph which he kept for the rest of his life, showing colleagues at the Amersham garage many years later. In fact it became something of a joke among staff and some 60 years after the event they re-enacted the scene using a later bus and a much older Wilf! The subsequent photograph was used to publicise a 1980's Amersham garage open day.

A further photo from this series of personal snaps features A&D driver Jim Chapman (white dust coat) and conductor Colin Hunt. The two were standing in front of Lancia bonnet no. 4. This Lancia model dated from 1926 and the photo was taken in 1928. Repairs to the bus and its final sell off date in January 1933 were recorded in the Company's minute books.

Jim had actually been engaged to drive one-man-operated buses for the company back in 1925 and this he continued to do, almost without exception, for the rest of his working life. He built up fantastic relations with his passengers and loved his job. Jim's son Peter recalls one of his dad's favourite tales; Jim was driving an Oldsmobile in the dark along the road to Cholesbury when the bus suddenly ground to a halt. He felt he had an idea of what might be wrong but needed the help of a couple of passengers in holding some lights so he might see what he was doing. All went well and to everyone's delight, Jim got them under way again and safely home that night. Earlier in this book there is an account of the tragic death at Ley Hill of Harvey Joiner, aged 8, very sadly for Jim he was the driver that day and although no blame was ever attached to him in the accident, his son said he almost never spoke about it for the rest of his life. Baring this dreadful incident Jim clearly enjoyed his time with A&D and in some of the photographs in this book can be seen driving on weekend excursions, always a favourite of his.

Photo Ernie Revel collection

Taken outside The Pheasant P.H. at Chalfont St. Giles is another of these treasured personal photos, this time saved for years by Ernie Revel. Here he is seen on his conductor duties running the Windsor to Chesham route in this 1929 Gilford (KX2595), A&D bonnet no. 27. Ernie is recorded as remembering that running this particular vehicle on that route was a very rare event. His driver can be seen peering from the top opening section of his windscreen and straining to get in the photograph. These soft top coaches were more versatile replacements for the old-style charabancs but in this case it was being used on regular bus duties.

Brown family photograph 1930

Following Amersham & District bus driver Albert (Bert) Brown's torrid period of luck reported in Chapter 5, it is wonderful to report that on Tuesday 4th March 1930 he married Miss Edith Arman at Amersham Parish Church. As the happy couple stepped out in the open they had to pass under a ceremonial arch of A&D bus destination "slip boards". These were held aloft by Bert's cheering colleagues from the garage. Emerging from the tunnel other guests showered Edith and Bert in "conductor's confetti", the colourful clippings from old punched bus tickets. These had been carefully saved in the weeks before the big day. Bert's workmates also clubbed together and bought them a canteen of cutlery.

Training drivers was another task undertaken by some of the old hands. This photograph taken at Ley Hill shows Wilf Brackley (centre) with trainee driver Charlie Bowens (right) and conductor for the day, John Mitchell (left).
Photo J Hutchinson collection.

GROWTH IN THE FINAL MONTHS

The Company was now moving forward in leaps and bounds and financial year 1931/2 proved to be another big one in their history. A year in which they bought a further five new vehicles; three AEC Regals and two Dennis's as well as completed their first competitor takeover!

Of the two new Dennis buses purchased, the first was an 18-seater GL model and this was put to work out of Chesham on the route to Aylesbury via Amersham, Great Missenden and Wendover.

KX8569 Dennis GL 18-seater model bought new in May 1932 and given A&D bonnet no. 1. To the rear of the vehicle the cinema commissionaire in frock coat and side striped trousers looks extremely dapper and could almost be confused with a bus inspector.
Photo J F Higham taken in 1933 courtesy of the A B Cross collection.

As we have already seen, A&D re-used bonnet numbers that had been relinquished by former vehicles and this bus was given the cherished no. 1 that had long since been surrendered but held back for some reason. (See Appendix 1 page 87 for a list of the known vehicles in use by A&D through the different stages of their history).

The second Dennis purchased, again in May 1932, was a 32-seat model called the Lancet and this was given bonnet no. 2. In the photograph overleaf it is shown at The Fountain, Frogmore, High Wycombe waiting for its return journey to Ley Hill. The Lancet was a competitor to the AEC Regal and we can compare the different Strachan bodies in the next two photographs. They are of the nearly new Lancet and a brand new Regal.

KX8570 Dennis Lancet A&D bonnet no.2 purchased in 1932.
Photo taken by J F Higham courtesy of the A B Cross collection.

One of a pair of luxurious AEC Regal coaches purchased by A&D, this one was registered KX8643 and issued with A&D bonnet no 7. Seen here, brand new at Strachans, awaiting delivery to the Company again for May 1932. Photo W Randall collection.

In June 1932 High Wycombe Council decided they didn't want buses to wait longer than 3 minutes at the stands on Frogmore or Queen Victoria Road; this came as a complete shock to the A&D Board. However, the directors saw it as an opportunity; the Secretary was instructed to write to other affected bus companies to offer them forecourt standing space to the side of the Company's new garage at the foot of Marlow Hill. Obviously there would be an appropriate charge should the offer be taken up. Details are unclear on how long this direction from the Council remained in place but certainly some competitors did pay A&D for the new standing space; periodically the nearby hospital also stood ambulances there.

In September the lucky inspector from the High Wycombe garage was supplied with an Austin 7 car, though the accounts only record a cost of £21. Probably the deposit payment!

A Boxing Hall?

In October 1932 the local Amersham & District Boxing Club asked to use one of the bus garages on The Broadway as an occasional venue for boxing contests. The directors discussed the matter at their next Board meeting and approved it for a charge of One Guinea (£1/1/-) per evening. Dr H J Henderson, an A&D director and local surgeon, was a keen supporter of the local boxing club.

Also at this time the Company introduced charges for dogs travelling on their buses, the rate to be half the adult fare. In addition they would also offer an unaccompanied parcel carrying service, to be administered by the conductor (see Appendix 2 for more details and charges). Petrol had just gone up from 10½d a gallon to 13½d a gallon. This is a huge percentage increase so maybe it is apparent why the Board were looking to squeeze extra revenue from any source.

The takeover of the Chesham & District Bus Company

The Chesham and District Bus Company (C&D) was based out of Nashleigh Hill Garage and founded by four director shareholders and a shareholding secretary named Florence Clay. They first advertised a bus service to Watford on 10th January 1930; it undertook 3 return journeys on Tuesdays and Saturdays for 1/9 a passenger. However, within 12 months, two directors and the secretary decided to sell their shares and resign, a new secretary was appointed and he put in a personal loan of £75 to the company.

In May 1931 A&D complained to C&D that they were not sticking to the timetable on the Great Missenden route. Not adhering to timetables is usually code for operating a route in a so-called "pirate" manner, by seeking to chase other operators and beat them to their scheduled stops in order to poach passengers. This is a practice that had been rife for a number of years.

By the end of 1931 Charles and Alfred Law had both bought 350 shares in C&D at £1 per share and gained control of the company. The fortunes of which did not improve; their minutes show they are always late paying bills, being beset by cash flow problems. The Traffic Commissioners were the current regulatory body and they had licenced C&D to run five local routes. The Company somehow managed to operate with an equal number of buses, all of which were on finance agreements that required prompt monthly payments to avoid being repossessed.

On 21st September 1932 LGOC learned that C&D was up for sale, they alerted the A&D Board and stated that they would agree to advance them funds with which to purchase the company if the A&D Board approved such an action. The Board decided the Chairman and Manager (C.Ivins and W.Randall) should make an appointment to meet with the directors of C&D. On 19th October Will Randall offered them £2,250 for the business as well as taking on the liability of the five vehicles at £1,658/2/6. This offer was refused.

Things must have gone from bad to worse for C&D, as on 23rd November the A&D Board recorded that Mr Law had accepted their even lower offer of £1774 for the company plus taking on the liability, now £1476/12/7, for the vehicles. The A&D Company seal was placed on the agreement on 14th December 1932, thus completing the only takeover of another company during their 14 years trading. The A&D Board and management continued to run C&D as a separate company until June 1933 when all licences were renewed in A&D's name.

A lovely period photo of Red Lion corner, Chesham and little 14-seater Chevrolet KX6513 (acquired by A&D in their takeover of Chesham & District).
Photograph courtesy Peter Hawkes, R East collection.

It was recorded in the Christmas Edition of The Bucks Examiner that a well known driver with Amersham and District had died aged just 44. He was William Frederick Edward Sydney of "Broadview" Chequers Hill, Amersham. Before joining the bus company William had been a chauffeur to Mr E.T. Tyrwhitt-Drake.

A Sports Club is formed

During 1932 the staff had formed a Sports Club to play football, cricket and tennis. The 1932/3 football season proved very successful with their team reaching two cup semi-finals. On Boxing Day 1932 the Amersham and District Bus Co. Football Club played the Penn Bus Co. team in a charity match, and A&D beat them 5-1.

At the beginning of February 1933 the football club held the first of many dances in The British Legion Hall, Whieldon St. The posters advertising the event proclaimed **"Girls! Your favourite**

conductor and driver will be there." It was a roaring success with 200 people attending, including Will Randall and some directors. Clearly the turnout spoke volumes for the good looking chaps employed by the bus company!

Step forward the fair haired dancing conductor – be my Valentine!

According to a report in the local press, on the 14th of the month a card was delivered addressed to **"Conductor, fair hair, good dancer"** c/o The Bus Company, Amersham, Bucks. The card was rapidly claimed at the depot and it is hoped a happy romance ensued but no doubt a lot of leg pulling and elbow nudging echoed around the garage.

A&D were still pressing ahead expanding their operations. In January 1933, at a Traffic Commissioner's hearing in Reading the Company was granted a licence to operate a route from Chesham to Beaconsfield, via Annes Corner (sic), Stanley Hill and Coleshill. Mr King-Hamilton appeared for the Company and explained that for a period between 1925 and 1926 they had operated a similar route taking in Seer Green. The Company thought a fresh direct service between Chesham and Beaconsfield was again needed and Amersham Parish Council supported their application. The service licence for eight return journeys every day Monday through to Saturday and five on Sundays was granted.

Shown above is the very last vehicle purchased by the Company. Like several other photographs used in this book, the coach can be seen brand new outside Strachan's Acton factory building. Unusually for this time it was a Gilford, registered ABH366 a 1933 model AS6 20-seater, looking very luxurious with curtains at the windows. It was possibly ordered by A&D to match the two AS6 vehicles inherited from the Chesham and District takeover. The coach was given A&D bonnet no. 38. The vehicle appears to be finished in the London General Country Bus green & black colour scheme and lacks the A&D name, possibly anticipating events soon to unfold.
Photo John Hutchinson collection.

69

Since 1929 there had been proposals to reform public transport in and around London, with a view to provide unification of services and place them under public control. Frank Pick was at the heart of these discussions and seemingly got on well with the Minister for Transport. For the first time, operators of buses and trains would work far more closely together. A bill called "The London Passenger Transport Bill" was passed and finally received Royal Assent on 13th April 1933. A new authority was created on 1st July named the "London Passenger Transport Board" but to be known as "London Transport". Frank Pick became the first Chief Executive Officer. The Board was given a virtual monopoly on operating road passenger transport across a 25 – 30 mile radius from the centre of the capital. Most independent operators in this area sold out to them in the months that followed, but the LPTB was empowered to grant permission for some other operators to remain in smaller pocket areas. Frank Pick actually favoured taking over operators who didn't want to reach voluntary agreement. The LGOC in turn offered A&D shareholders £3/5/0 for each of their shares and the directors an additional £2,500 (equal to 3 years worth of fees) as compensation. The offer was recommended to the shareholders. On 28th June 1933 Chas. Ivins, A&D Chairman, was asked to wind up Amersham & District Motor Bus Co. and act as liquidator. A&D was already financially controlled by the new LTPB and became fully absorbed into the fold on 1st October 1933. As might be imagined this was not necessarily welcomed by all sections of the public, many of whom had a fondness for the "old" original Amersham and District buses and generally favoured small operators over big conglomerates.

However, the staff went to work one day for the old and much loved Amersham & District Bus Co. and the next they were employed by London Transport (LT). Administration staff still dealt with all the Company's old clients who hired buses, even recording them as A&D sales well into 1934, possibly until the end of the normal A&D financial year. As an example, Chesham United F.C. paid £2/5/0 to have 18 passengers taken to Aylesbury and back (44 miles recorded) on 24th March 1934. The old Amersham & District office sign remained in place for many months and must have given some feeling of comfort that things hadn't totally altered.

The A&D vehicle fleet comprising 43 buses and 5 coaches was finally transferred to London Transport on 24th November 1933. All A&D vehicle stock acquired at this time was fully inspected and old or non-compatible - largely anything not manufactured by AEC - was disposed of over the next few years. London Transport would now embark on mass produced standardisation, the lovely hand-crafted vehicles individually ordered with their adornments born from a graceful era will be set aside and pass into the recesses of memory. However, this did not happen overnight and LT needed to phase out the use of the eclectic mix of vehicles they had acquired. The very early ex-solid tyred vehicles went almost immediately and the rest were shuffled around into different areas according to their original manufacturer. Amersham was about to lose its Gilfords but gained more Dennis vehicles. Those being retained were repainted in LT's country area green with black side stripes, some could be seen with the old "GENERAL" or "GENERAL Country Services" branding but this was soon changed again to display the new "London Transport" logo.

Sadly some buses that had given great service over A&D's history were left to languish and await their fate at the auctions or scrap yards. A few of their potted histories are told in the next chapter but the two photographs opposite paint their own poignant pictures.

This is a photograph of our old familiar friend, the 1925 Dennis PP3477 still proudly wearing no. 9 on her bonnet. She is parked in one of A&D's garages, seemingly lifeless and one-eyed, waiting to be towed to her fate by something more modern.
Throughout this book we have followed the various phases in the life of no. 9 and now she passes into history at the same time as the Company itself.
Photo taken in 1934 by the late D W K Jones, courtesy of A D Packer collection.

Photo J Hutchinson collection.

This book opened with a line penned by Laurie Lee "white roads innocent of oil and petrol" and sadly we can see from this photograph taken in front of The Crown at Ley Hill, the roads were now heavily stained. However, we must reflect on the change brought about by the very technological advancement depicted through these pages. The humble omnibus had brought a new found freedom of travel to thousands who had previously barely set foot outside of their local area. People benefitted from seeking improved employment further afield, children were able to travel to better schools and enhance their education. Our countryside scenes of pastoral serenity remained largely unmolested, the beautiful childhood nostalgia for cloudless summers would continue. However, in tandem with home electricity and the wireless, the coming of wide spread bus services brought the population into the modern era. The petrol engine that, years before, had been cast as the villain had perhaps atoned for a few of its sins.

THE MEMORIES OF A&D LINGERED ON...

The local bus company that had made such a tentative start and had grown to become one of the largest independent operators on the outskirts of London had ceased. The A&D name so familiar among the towns and villages of South Buckinghamshire was gone forever and a new dawn began for London Transport. A big new bus garage was soon built in Old Amersham; Will Randall played a major part; the Second World War saw massive upheaval; passenger numbers continued to rise for another 20 years and queues for Sunday buses home from Chiltern beauty spots became a common sight, but all this is another story waiting to be told. However, memories of the old firm lingered longer.

Will Randall wasn't too pleased with the takeover by the London Passenger Transport Board but he rose to prominence within that organisation and became District Superintendant of the Western District of the Country Bus and Coach section. This was formed out of the old A&D area of operation with the old A&D offices designated as the new District Office.

By 1939 Will was living at "Waycroft", Long Park, Chesham Bois, the property where he was to stay for the rest of his life. He retired in 1947, aged just 55 but on grounds of ill health. Will had been on sick leave since December 1945; he had spent all 28 years of his service in the Amersham district. His health deteriorated with diabetes and blindness, his granddaughter remembers reading the newspapers to him in the 1950's and helping him with his horse racing selections; a pastime not exactly approved of by his wife. Will passed away on 5th August 1956, having not yet reached the official retirement age of 65. In a notice in the Bucks Examiner, Will's family thanked Dr. Starkey, the other doctors and nursing staff at Amersham Hospital for all their kindness. Will Randall is buried in Penn cemetery.

Charles Ivins, Chairman and founding Director of the company carried on running The Station Hotel, Amersham for some time (he also had interests in other hostelries around the area). Charles died aged 76 at The Grand Hotel, Brighton in 1953. He had a grandson (Stewart) who, many years later, ran a local coach business bearing the "Pride of Bucks" name.

Dr H J Henderson, Director, retired to Bexhill on Sea and died in 1953.

Percy Hounslow thoroughly enjoyed his time as an A&D conductor, but at the end of 1933 he left to become a driver with Thames Valley Motor Bus Co. He finished his career on the buses as Chief Inspector with that company.

Jim Chapman, **Wilf Brackley** and **Ernie Revel** spent many years longer in the service of London Transport with Jim finally stepping down from the cab in October 1969 over 44 years after Will Randall had offered him the job, Jim's daughter-in-law described him as a "Good old Bucks gentleman". Jim, Wilf and Ernie went on to keep in touch with staff at the Amersham Garage and some of their handed down material has helped create this book.

John Merrell has so far not been mentioned in the book but he had moved to the area to become an A&D driver; initially lodging with another employee of the company, Jack Archer. John ended up becoming Jim Chapman's brother-in-law as he married his wife's sister; yet another marriage through the conduit of A&D! John is seen in the following photograph wearing a London Transport uniform; therefore it must have been taken around 1934 and before the old A&D office signage was changed.

John Merrell, former A&D driver posing on his pride and joy outside the Head Office.
The Chapman family collection

The Sports and Social Club went from strength to strength and still got regular mention in the local press. In February 1934 a fancy dress party was held at the Amersham British Legion hall and Miss D Bedford as Miss Killjoy and Mr Driver Rutland (sic) as D.O.R.A were voted the best dressed. One year later a party for the busmen's children was arranged, again at the British Legion hall. For weeks the employees had been raising funds by placing loose coins in a box at the Amersham garage. Mr Godbold was the M.C., usher, announcer and mirth-maker, ably supported by a Punch and Judy show and a "movie". That same night the Sports Club organised a dance for the mothers and fathers, Mr H Goss was M.C. for the evening. In May 1935 it was reported that teams of ten busmen from Amersham and High Wycombe garages met in a tennis match. Amersham triumphed by 51 to 42 games. So the fun went on.

WHAT HAPPENED TO THE OLD A&D VEHICLES?

As already mentioned some vehicles were disposed of almost immediately, whilst others worked on for a period of time. The very early Dennis 2.5 ton vehicles were disposed of in the months following the take-over; the smaller Dennis GL's were withdrawn in 1935 and the Dennis E's in 1936. The Gilfords were all sold on by the end of 1937. The AEC Regals T69, T71, T89, T96, T104, T365 and T366 lasted until 1938/9, but the better ones went on beyond WW2, see details and photos below. T104 saw service with the Royal Air Force from 1942-7. The two double-deck AEC Regents also soldiered on into the 1950's!

A photograph thought to be taken at the rear of the Amersham premises shows the diminutive 1927 PP7700 Dennis 30cwt 14-seater, by this time repainted in London General colours it was disposed of in October 1934. The larger vehicle on the left has registration HW1623, but was not one of A&D's former buses.

Photo by the late D W K Jones, courtesy of A D Packer collection.

KX470, A&D no. 15, the lovely all-weather Dennis F coach, previously seen with proud driver Jim Chapman, is photographed languishing in a scrap yard in January 1935 where it was broken up; still less than 7 years old! Withdrawn from Amersham in 1934 it was sold off by London Transport that October along with the other A&D Gilford all-weather coaches nos. 27 and 31.

Photo by the late D W K Jones, courtesy of A D Packer collection.

KX6513 Chevrolet U 14-seater built 1931, it joined the A&D fleet in November 1932 following the takeover of Chesham & District Bus Co. and was given bonnet no. 39. The (later fitted) destination board is set for Berkhamsted. Records show this vehicle was withdrawn almost immediately in 1934; it was later converted to a lorry by its new owners.
Photo by the late D W K Jones, courtesy of A D Packer collection.

KX5923 formerly A&D no. 32, Dennis GL 18-seater, seen here in Chesham on the 369A route in May 1935. She was sold off by London Transport exactly one year later.
Photo by the late D W K Jones, courtesy of A D Packer collection.

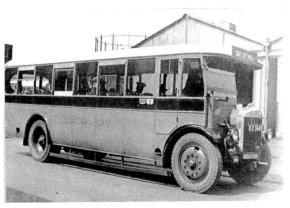

KX1645 Dennis E formerly bonnet no. 18, seen at the Amersham garage after the takeover. On board are passengers ready for the continuation of route 362 to Chesham and then up to Ley Hill. All the old A&D Dennis E's were disposed of early in 1936.

PP7144 Dennis 2.5 ton 1926 formerly bonnet no. 6 which is still just visible. Photographed in front of the old A&D garages shortly after the takeover, it has been sprayed green and black but has no General or London Transport markings. It didn't last long with LT and was sold in April 1936.
Photo by the late D W K Jones, courtesy of A D Packer collection.

ABH366 a 1933 20-seat AS6 model Gilford, originally A&D bonnet no. 38, was the last ever vehicle purchased by A&D and seen earlier in this book outside the Strachan factory. Here it is painted red and operating for London Transport as GF194 in Purley, it did this between August 1935 and being sold in June 1936, just 3 years old.
Photo taken by J F Higham courtesy of A B Cross collection

KX8570 Dennis Lancet ex A&D bonnet no. 2, seen here in London General livery shortly after the takeover and ready for its return journey to Ley Hill. It was later given the LT bonnet no. DT3 and also transferred to Hemel Hempstead for duties on the 337 Studham route. It was sold off in November 1937.
Photo taken by J F Higham courtesy of A B Cross collection

KX8644 formerly A&D bonnet no. 4, subsequently given LT designation T366, photographed outside the newly branded London Transport office. This vehicle was retired from service by LT in 1939 along with A&D bonnet no. 7 (T365).
Photo courtesy of The Kithead Trust

Oh, how things can change, KX8644 (ex T366 as seen previously) now looks like this, resplendent with a smart Duple body fitted in 1939, she saw service with the Royal Navy in WW2. Photographed at the Epsom Derby on 4th June 1949 operated by the Overland coach company.
Photograph courtesy of the A B Cross collection.

KX7634 last seen as A&D 36 with Wilf Brackley at Ley Hill and a pool of oil in front of her, she has been given a GREENLINE make over for 1934 and become T361, photographed in front of the old A&D Company offices.
Photograph courtesy of the A B Cross collection.

KX7634 (T361) now showing off and out manoeuvring trams by The Horns, Kennington. Photograph P J Marshall courtesy of A B Cross collection.

We surely couldn't leave the story of KX7634 without including this shot taken on 18th May 1950 in Watford. Her bodywork having been totally replaced in 1938 with a metal framed one by Weymann. Along with T359 and T362 in 1942 she had her interior lay-out changed; the seats were moved down the sides of the bus in order to accommodate standing passengers as war-time demands required her to carry more people to work. The normal layout was restored after 1945. She finally stopped working for LT in 1953 and operated in the Wolverhampton area until at least November 1959. Great continuous service for an AEC Regal bought new in 1931 by Amersham & District. T359, T362 and T364 were also sold off by LT in 1953.
Photograph R Hobbs courtesy of A B Cross collection.

KX4656 ex. A&D no. 29 seen working for London Transport Country Buses (now numbered ST1089) and sporting their green and black livery. Wilf Brackley at the wheel and parked at Berkhamsted.
Photo J Hutchinson collection.

Several years later but KX4656 can still be seen in Chesham Broadway, this time in wintry sleet conditions. Photograph probably taken just before WW2. KX4656 was sold off on 27th March 1953 exactly 23 years since joining the A&D fleet. It was scrapped in 1954.
Photograph J F Higham courtesy of A B Cross collection.

KX5055 ex A&D no. 30 now LT's ST1090 seen at the Nashleigh Hill, Chesham turn around point for the 336. This vehicle has undergone some body modifications, especially to the front upper deck. Photograph taken around 1947/8.
Photograph credited to D.A. Thompson.

KX5055 spent some time in the evening of its life working the 230 route in the Harrow area. It was finally sold to a dealer in Leeds for scrap in February 1953 having joined A&D in May 1930. It was in 1952 that the author moved to Kenton (Harrow) and started many years of travelling on the 230.
Photograph credited to C Carter courtesy of A B Cross collection

SAFETY FIRST DRIVING AWARDS

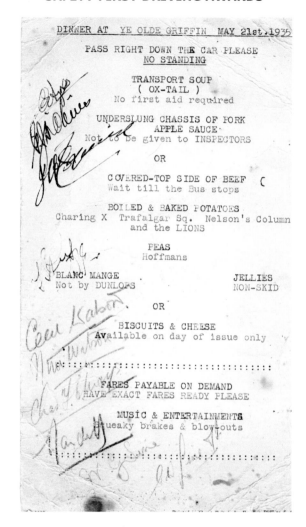

Dinner at Ye Olde Griffin May 21st 1935 – signed menu card from the event.

On Tuesday 21st May, forty-four Safety First Awards were issued to LPTB drivers from Amersham and High Wycombe garages for their driving during 1934. The presentations were made by C E Ayres, the Operating Superintendant of Country Buses based at Reigate; his Operating Assistant J G Dickins; W Randall, District Superintendant; District Inspectors G Line and C Mays. Mr Ayres gave an impassioned speech extolling how being extra diligent whilst driving inevitably made for better and safer drivers. Reducing accidents was of paramount importance to the Company, only the day previously a bad accident had been reported from Ware. He singled out F Church for special mention; he had been driving buses from High Wycombe since 1929, averaging 50,000 miles each year without any blameworthy accidents. Mr Church was awarded a "Silver Bar" to his previous awards. He had his first Safety First Diploma awarded in 1927 when still a lorry driver and he thought he had driven over 1.7 million miles since.

Various toasts were proposed; Mr Randall proposed one for the Chairman and in return he proposed one for Mr Randall. Will Randall must have been especially pleased with the way things were turning out, he was now in a senior position for one of the world's largest bus fleet operators and here he was sitting back in The Griffin Hotel, Amersham where the story had begun 16 years earlier. Not withstanding the fact he was again surrounded by his "lads" who were now doing so well under their new employers.

The menu caused a lot of good humour, with appended remarks typed out for each course. Near the end it said "Fares Payable on Demand" this referred to the diners individual drinks bills! Music and Entertainment came from Mr and Mrs Cecil Watson. Mr J H Squire, violoncello player of Wireless Celeste Octette fame also entertained, Mr Squire was supported by Frank M Reade. Mr H Godbold, an untiring worker at social events, was a welcome soloist, and the same can be said to apply to Mr W T Castle, Mr J Chapman and Mr W Brackley. Quite a novel entertainment was also provided by Mr W Jones on the piano-accordion.

THE AWARDS

Diplomas were awarded to:-
AMERSHAM
F Hurst, T Swadling, W J Chapman, F J Brown, W Hance, D Mulkern, S W Francis, L J Harris, W A Brown, R J Merrell, R Simpkins, W Dyer, J Skells, W J Brackley, P C Brazier, F Branham, H A Hall, F G J Rays, R F Mayo, H Rutland, C J W Bowers, R J Williams, A E Halls, S H Reading.
HIGH WYCOMBE
F Church (Silver bar), F E Beale, H Bickmore, P H Dean, C T Fletcher, R G E Gay, J Hartley, G T Honeyman, J Howson, F J Jemmett, S J Mathews, C Meadows, A H Newell, H Perry, H L Purves, C Queen, A F Shrimpton, M Townson, F A H Wright, G H Scott.

The signatures on the menu card are as follows:-
Top-bottom
C E Ayres, Operating Superintendant of Country Buses based at Reigate.
(Possibly) C J W Bowers, driver Amersham.
J H Squire, entertainer.
Not indentified.
Mr Cecil Watson, entertainer.
Mrs Watson, entertainer.
Chas Mays, District Inspector.
W Randall, District Superintendant based at Amersham.
Mr G Line, District Inspector.
(Possibly) Mrs Line
H Godbold has signed on the reverse, Amersham employee and soloist entertainer.

Clearly a lot of effort went into dreaming up all the anecdotes under each course and we can only image that many stories were re-lived that night, some of which may well have been told in this book. It can be safely assumed that the vast majority of the drivers honoured that night were former A&D employees, we can of course recognise a number of the names from mention throughout this book.

MORE THAN 15 YEARS LATER ....

A column in the Bucks Examiner reported on the LT Amersham Garage for the 1949 North-West Area of London Transport Country Buses Safe Driver Awards as follows:-

"It is interesting to note that those who have known this garage from the old days of the A&D - the local bus service - that many of the old A&D men of those days figure in the 1949 awards, and those that receive the 11-14 years Oak Leaf Bars will recall the old days and their merry events inseparable from a pioneer service. Some of those men of the old days have gone, alas, and this list inevitably recalls them.

J C Archer, W J Brackley, W A Brown, W J Chapman, W M Dyer, E W J Easton, B W Francis, A Gurney, A W Harrowell, T Hoard, J Machin, D H Mulkern, W R Pattison, R A Richardson, T F Stictland and R W Walton".
"5 year Medal - E J Revel."
As it was now 16 years since the "old A&D" was taken over not all the men listed above will have actually served for the company, however, we continue to recognise some of the names and it is clear from the report that the original bus company for the area was still held in high regard.

Amazingly right up 1968 London Transport's Amersham bus garage still operated using the old A&D telephone number of Amersham 36. The 1969 telephone directory then lists it as Amersham 4636.

The remaining old A&D garages and head office block in Amersham had for decades been used as a car sales and repair outlet. However, by January 2017 they were facing demolition. Two colleagues and I were allowed to go up into the top floor front office, presumably the one used by Will Randall all those years ago. The clock on the outside wall was long gone, but it had revealed a pretty round window through which this photograph was taken, a view of old Amersham cottages that would have greeted Will every time he looked out from either of his front windows. Efforts were made to have these buildings relocated to either The Chiltern Open Air Museum or The Brooklands Museum, but neither materialised. A&D's former High Wycombe garage does still survive as home to a major office stationary outlet.

Just as this book was going to print, on 11th May 2017 the sentence was carried out *in-camera*. From behind blue hoarding and showing no mercy, the mechanical T. Rexes of the demolition death squad surrounded their prey. In no time their metal and brick eating jaws had reduced to rubble the buildings that, a little under 90 years earlier, had been an up-to-date hub for wider social mobility. The spirits of Will Randall and Charles Ivins will have repaired to the tranquillity of The Griffin to mull over the days developments and wash the dust from their throats. Another chapter had ended for their old firm.

BEFORE YOU FINALLY GO

There have been a few small "back" stories running through this book, the pictorial history of number 9, probably being the most memorable. I had always wanted to include a photograph of an old A&D vehicle out labouring away somewhere in the leafy Chiltern lanes, so imagine my surprise when, two years into this research, I was handed a thin file that had languished in John Hutchinson's loft since the 1980's. It contained the very photo I had craved. Even further excitement ensued when a magnifying glass revealed the registration plate to be that of number 9 making its way up from Chesham to Amersham, this photograph is reproduced in Chapter 4. Now, if that wasn't coincidence enough also in the folder was an envelope that contained half a dozen "National Safety First Association" driver "Diplomas" and the menu card reproduced on page 82. The diploma was issued to a driver free from blameworthy accidents. The six certificates dated between 1933 and 1940 were all issued to William James Chapman (Jim) with him receiving the 1934 at the special Griffin dinner.

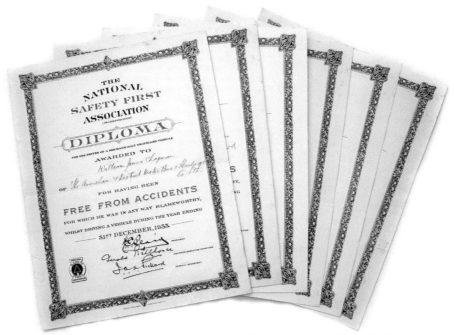

Six of Jim Chapman's surviving National Safety First Diploma's.
Courtesy John Hutchinson collection.

Jim's A&D career has been mentioned many times in this book. Jim's son (Pete) and daughter-in-law (Linda) had been the only people to contact me following a plea for information placed in a local Chesham magazine. His father's personal photographs have added greatly to our knowledge of the Company and many now enhance this book. Amazingly Pete and Linda also still had two original letters written by Will Randall in 1925 offering Jim his driving job with the Company. At my first meeting with them I explained how my interest in the Amersham & District Bus Company had been sparked by researching the tragic and fatal 1930 accident in my village of Ley Hill (see Foreword and Chapter 5). Utter surprise came when he told me that it was his father driving the bus that day. I had been keen on finding a photograph of the Gilford bus involved, but Jim's collection, not unsurprisingly, didn't help. Who would want to keep a photograph of a vehicle where the memories would have been so painful? Another coincidence was about to occur when, some 85 years after that incident, a single photograph has now turned up of the rather unique vehicle involved that day. It had recently been handed in to the Amersham Museum by the son of Percy Hounslow, a former conductor for A&D. Percy's son would have no inkling on the significance of this tiny 1930's black and white image among his late father's album of memories.

This photograph taken at Queen Victoria Ave., High Wycombe shows Gilford KX3928 A&D bonnet no. 8 with its two doorways, unique to the company.
Photo courtesy of Amersham Museum, Percy Hounslow collection.

We know from Jim's son that his father never talked about the dreadful accident. Now, on seeing the Percy Hounslow photograph and realising how the closed doors at the top of the little staircases combined with a lack of mirrors on the vehicle could allow the boys to duck down out of sight and play the prank they did. The coroner never in any way thought the driver or conductor were to blame and so the original story ended with the inquest. Were these extra pieces of the jigsaw for Jim Chapman's life sheer coincidence in my research? I think that dark day in April 1930 played on Jim's mind for the rest of his life and he went on working hard to show how good a driver he was, even still gaining mention as such in the Bucks Examiner 20 years later. At the opening of this book I dedicated it to the memory of Harvey Joiner, but two people suffered profoundly that day and I have no hesitation in also dedicating it to the memory of Jim Chapman, clearly an outstanding driver.

APPENDIX 1 - AMERSHAM & DISTRICT BUS AND COACH FLEET 1919-1933

Reg. No.	A&D No.	LT no.	Make	Model	Body	Seats	Decks	New?	Built	Date Regist'd or into service	Cost £	Date out of stock
BH0158			Scout	32HP	Hodson	26	S/D	S/H		24-May-19	875	Feb-21
BH0193			Scout	32HP		26	S/D	S/H		17-Jul-19	875	Sep-21
BH0157			AEC	3 ton	Hodson	26	S/D	S/H	1916	15-May-19	1440	Mar-26
BH9306	4		Oldsmobile		Hodson	B14F	S/D	New	1922	Jul-22	440	1927
PP268			Crossley			14	S/D	S/H	1919	May-23	482	1928
unknown			GMC Sal.	20hp Station bus		14	S/D	S/H	?	1924	185	1926
PP1344	7		Oldsmobile		Strachan	B14F	S/D	New	1924	Feb-24	417	
unknown	8		Oldsmobile			14	S/D			1924		pre Aug25
PP3477	9		Dennis	3.4 ton	Strachan	B29R	S/D	New	1925	Mar-25	1123	Nov-33
PP4089	10		Dennis	2.5ton	Strachan	B29R	S/D	New	1925	23-May-25	1100	Nov-33
unknown	not issued		Oldsmobile		Got GMC body	14	S/D	S/H	?	Sep-25	32	
PP5254	11		Dennis	2.5ton	Strachan	B26F	S/D	New	1926	30-Jan-26	1095	Nov-33
PP5454	12		Dennis	2.5ton	Strachan	B26F	S/D	New	1926	08-Feb-26	1035	Nov-33
PP7144	6		Dennis	2.5ton	Strachan	B30R	S/D	New	1926	13-Nov-26	1115	Nov-33
PP7251	3		Dennis	2.5ton	Strachan	B26R	S/D	New	1926	11-Dec-26		Nov-33
HX6543?	4		Lancia		Strachan	B18F	S/D	New	1926	Dec-26	1005	Jan-33
PP7700	14		Dennis	30cwt	Strachan	B14F	S/D	New	1927	16-Mar-27	582	Nov-33
PP9954	16		Dennis	E	Strachan	B32	S/D	New	1928	Mar-28	1328	Nov-33
KX470	15		Dennis	F	Strachan A-W	C30R	S/D	New	1928	07-May-28	1272	Nov-33
KX1195			Chevrolet	LP		B14F	S/D			1928	Sep-28	330	pre Nov33
KX1326	13		Dennis	G	Strachan	B18F	S/D	New	1928	Oct-28		Nov-33
KX1580	5		Chevrolet	LP	Wilmott	B14F	S/D	New	1928	Dec-28	405	Nov-33
KX1645	18		Dennis	E	Strachan	B32F	S/D	New	1928	29-Dec-28		Nov-33
KX1923	17	GF161	Gilford	166OT	Strachan	B32R	S/D	New	1929	Feb-29		Nov-33
KX1924	19		Dennis	E	Strachan	B32R	S/D	New	1929	Feb-29		Nov-33
KX1925	23		Dennis	E	Strachan	B32R	S/D	New	1929	Feb-29		Nov-33
KX1926	20		Dennis	E	Strachan	B32R	S/D	New	1929	Feb-29		Nov-33
KX1928	22		Dennis	E	Strachan	B32R	S/D	New	1929	Feb-29		Nov-33
KX1927	25		Dennis	E	Strachan	B32R	S/D	New	1929	Feb-29		Nov-33
KX2219	24		Dennis	E	Strachan	B32R	S/D	New	1929	Mar-29		Nov-33
KX2595	27		Gilford	166SD	Strachan A-W	C30R	S/D	New	1929	May-29		Nov-33
KX2793	21		Dennis	E	Strachan	B32R	S/D	New	1929	May-29		Nov-33
KX2794	26		Dennis	E	Strachan	B32R	S/D	New	1929	May-29		Nov-33
KX3928	8	GF162	Gilford	168OT	Strachan	B32D	S/D	New	1930	Jan-30		Nov-33
KX4337	28		Dennis	EV	Strachan	B32R	S/D	New	1930	Mar-30		Nov-33
KX4656	29	ST1089	AEC	Regent lowb	Short Bros	48	D/D	New	1930	Apr-30		Nov-33
KX5055	30	ST1090	AEC	Regent lowb	Strachan	48	D/D	New	1930	May-30		Nov-33
KX4984	31		Gilford	168SD	Strachan A-W	C30R	S/D	New	1930	May-30		Nov-33
KX5923	32		Dennis	GL	Strachan	B18F	S/D	New	1930	Oct-30	chassis 435	Nov-33
KX5967	33		Dennis	GL	Strachan	B18F	S/D	New	1930	Nov-30	chassis 425	Nov-33
unknown	not issued		Guy				D/D	S/H		Jan-31	500	Mar-32
unknown	not issued		Guy				D/D	S/H		Jan-31	500	Mar-32
GF535	T69	T69	AEC	Regal	Chiswick	C27R	S/D	S/H	1930	Jan-31		Nov-33
GF536	T71	T71	AEC	Regal	Chiswick	C27R	S/D	S/H	1930	Jan-31		Nov-33
GF543	T89	T89	AEC	Regal	Chiswick	C27R	S/D	S/H	1930	Jan-31		Nov-33
GF544	T96	T96	AEC	Regal	Chiswick	C27R	S/D	S/H	1930	Jan-31		Nov-33
GF550	T104	T104	AEC	Regal	Short Bros	C27R	S/D	S/H	1930	Jan-31		Nov-33
HX1855	not issued		Gilford	AS6	Petty	B20D	S/D	S/H	1930	Nov-32		Nov-33
KX7164	not issued		Gilford	AS6	Petty	B20F	S/D	New	Jun-31	Nov-32	C&D £828	Nov-33
KX7469	41		AJS	Pilot	Petty	B20F	S/D	New	Aug-31	Nov-32		Nov-33
GO9046	40		Chevrolet	U	Thurgood	B14F	S/D	S/H	1931	Nov-32		Nov-33
KX6513	39		Chevrolet	U		B14F	S/D	S/H	1931	Nov-32		Nov-33
KX6785	34	T364	AEC	Regal	Strachan	C32R	S/D	New	1931	Apr-31		Nov-33
KX7635	35	T362	AEC	Regal	Strachan	C32R	S/D	New	1931	Oct-31	1500	Nov-33
KX7634	36	T361	AEC	Regal	Strachan	C32R	S/D	New	1931	Oct-31	1500	Nov-33
KX7886	37	T359	AEC	Regal	Strachan	C32R	S/D	New	1932	Dec-31	1450	Nov-33
KX8569	1		Dennis	GL	Strachan	B18F	S/D	New	1932	May-32	718	Nov-33
KX8570	2	DT3B	Dennis	Lancet	Strachan	B32R	S/D	New	1932	May-32	chassis 620	Nov-33
KX8643	7	T365	AEC	Regal	Strachan	C32R	S/D	New	1932	May-32	1440	Nov-33
KX8644	4	T366	AEC	Regal	Strachan	C32R	S/D	New	1932	May-32	1440	Nov-33
ABH366	38	GF194	Gilford	AS6	Strachan	B20F	S/D	New	1933	May-33	844	Nov-33
										Into LT stock 48 vehicles		

CHARABANCS

Reg. No.	A&D No.	LT no.	Make	Model	Body	Seats	Decks	New?	Built	Date Regist'd or into service	Cost £	Date out of stock
P3569	2		Dennis	Charabanc		28	S/D			1919	1600	
BH0348	1		Dennis	Chara 30HP	Roberts body	28	S/D	S/H	1920	10-May-20	body 350	Jan-31
BH 8331	3		Dennis	Charabanc	3 ton 16cwt	28	S/D	new	Oct-21	May-23		Sep-27
unknown	Fosters old one					28	S/D	S/H	1919?	Feb-28	160	

LORRIES

Reg. No.	A&D No.	LT no.	Make	Model	Body	Seats	Decks	New?	Built	Date Regist'd or into service	Cost £	Date out of stock
BH0157			AEC	3 ton 40 HP	Lorry service colour					15-May-19		
BH 8331			Dennis	3 ton 16 cwt	Green lorry				1921	11-Oct-21		

Notation on "Seats" column: B or C means Bus or Coach; number of seats; F, R or D means Front, Rear or Double entrance
A-W stands for All-Weather body

APPENDIX 2 - ROUTES AND ROUTE NUMBERING

Unlike a lot of major operators, A&D never displayed route numbers on their vehicles. The Company always only showed the final destination on the front of the bus and this would be changed at each turnaround point. From contemporary photographs most buses can be seen to have side boarding that displayed the various via points on route. Timetables were originally printed notices stuck on suitable spots adjacent to regular stopping places. In September 1925 the board gave permission to have proper weather resistant frames made and permanently fixed, displaying the up to date route information. Very occasionally the company would pay out to have timetables published in the local press. The Company went on to print very comprehensive bus timetable booklets during 1931 and 1932. Some pages from the February 1931 timetable are shown on these pages with no route numbers being used but in an August timetable of the same year, and seemingly for the first time, each route is given a number. In general the route numbers are consecutive numbers from the time the routes were started by the company, but this is not always the case.

Cover for the timetable booklet issued from 1st February 1931. (Size reduced)
Image courtesy of Amersham Museum

Image from inside the rear cover of the same booklet on the very back was an advert for Brandons similar to ones seen in the next chapter on their A&D ticket advertising.
Image courtesy of Amersham Museum

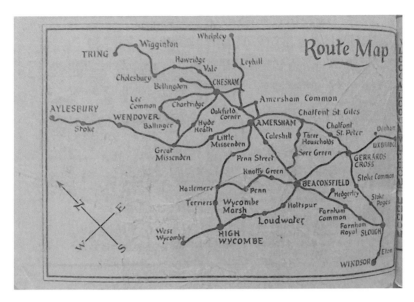

Inside the February 1931 booklet along with comprehensive route data on all daily and weekend bus times was this rather rudimentary map of the Company's services.
Image courtesy of Amersham Museum

THE
AMERSHAM & DISTRICT MOTOR BUS & HAULAGE Co. Ltd.

Registered Office—BROADWAY, AMERSHAM.　　　　'Phone—Amersham 56.

INDEX.

Also included was this index of routes, please note in this edition no numbers are allocated to the routes, but a in a similar timetable booklet published in August 1931 the Company gives each route a number.
Image courtesy of Amersham Museum

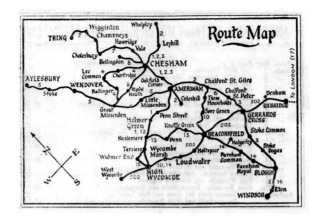

PASSENGER REGULATIONS.

THE AMERSHAM & DISTRICT MOTOR BUS & HAULAGE CO., LTD. give notice that they do not undertake that their vehicles shall start or arrive at the time specified in the Time Table, nor will they be accountable for any loss, inconvenience or injury arising from any cause.

Persons desirous of travelling to or from places at which no fare has been fixed, must pay the fare chargeable to or from the place beyond.

Children between 3 and 14, if not occupying a seat to the exclusion of other passengers, will be carried at half single fare. Minimum fare 1d. odd half-pennies above this amount counting as 1d. Half Threepenny fare 1½d. Odd Half-pennies above this amount counting as 1d.

Return tickets will be accepted but not issued on Bank Holidays.

Parcels carried at owners' risk.

The three pages above are reprinted from the A&D timetable dated 8 February 1932. Route numbers had been adopted in the August 1931 timetable but still did not appear on the vehicles. This booklet also contains more advertisements; a hairdressers in Harrow, Brandons, Bucks Insurance, Rust & Ratcliffe builders and George Knowles riding master (children's lessons a speciality!).
Images courtesy of Paul Dodge

This is a list of all the routes known to have been operated by the Company during their 14 years in business.

Route No.	Start Date	Notes	Destination
1	26/05/19	ii	Ley Hill-Chesham-Amersham-Holmer Green-High Wycombe
	22/03/20	i	Uxbridge-Amersham-Aylesbury
2		ii	Coleshill-Amersham-Chesham-Ley Hill-Whelpley Hill
3	04/08/22	ii	Ley Hill-Chesham-Amersham-Chalfonts-Gerrards X-Slough-Windsor
	1923	vii	Amersham-Holmer Green-Chalfont St Giles-Beaconsfield
4	04/05/25		Gt.Missenden-Ballinger-Lee Common-Chartridge-Chesham Moor
	1925	ix	Chesham-Amersham-Coleshill-Seer Grn-Beaconsfield
5	By May 28		Chesham-Amersham-Gt.Missenden-Wendover-Aylesbury
		iii	Extended via Chalfonts-GX-Windsor 4 Jul 1932
6	Jan 27		Gerrards X-Gold Hill-Chalfonts-Three Households
7	By May 28		Chesham-Cholesbury-Wigginton-Tring
8	By Aug 29	viii	Chesham-Hivings Hill-Bellingdon
9	By Aug 29	viii	Chesham-Fullers Hill-Hyde Heath
10	By Aug 29	viii	Gerrards X-Chalfonts-Three Households-Seer Green-Loudwater-High Wycombe
11			King Geo. V-Cricket Gnd-Church St.-Desborough Pk. Rd - (Wycombe local service)
12			Holmer Grn.-Hazlemere-Terriers-High Wycombe
13			High Wycombe-Hazlemere-Penn-Beaconsfield
14	March 30		High Wycombe-Beaconsfield-Farnham Common-Slough-Eton-Windsor
15			High Wycombe-Terriers-Widmer End
17	22/01/31	v	Chesham-Uxbridge-London (Express Coach Service)
502A	01/06/30		High Wycombe-Beaconsfield-Gerrards X-Denham-Uxbridge
			Inc. serv. Beaconsfield-New Town
			Inc. serv. Beaconsfield-Loudwater-High Wycombe
16	08/12/32	iv	Chesham-Lye Green-Bovingdon-Hemel Hempstead
18	08/12/32	iv	High Wycombe-Wooburn Green
19	08/12/32	iv	Gt. Missenden-Ltl. Missenden-Amersham-then as Route 3 to Windsor
20	13/01/33	vi	Chesham-Chesham Bois-Stanley Hill-Amersham Coleshill-Beaconsfield
21	08/12/32	iv	Chesham-Lye Green-Ashley Green-Berkhamsted
22	08/12/32	iv	Chesham-Hivings Hill-Pond Park Estate
23	Feb 1933	iv	Chesham-Amersham-Coleshill-Winchmore Hill-Tylers Green-Penn-Beaconsfield

NOTES
The route numbers used above were never displayed on vehicles and first appeared in a timetable dated 1st August 1931.
  i   Route ended September 1920 due to lack of custom.
  ii Routes extended to Ley Hill by November 1925.
  iii Start date as recorded in Company minute book.
  iv Routes operated by A&D following the takeover of Chesham & District.
  v   Start point became Amersham from 21st Oct 1931 as Traffic Commissioner disallowed starting from Chesham.
  vi Route reported in Bucks Examiner as being granted by Council on this date.
  vii According to A&D records this was the third route started, it was later absorbed into other services.
  viii The route was certainly in place by August 1929, actual start date not known.
  ix Route withdrawn 1926 but permission to re-start similar route given Jan 1933

AFTER THE TAKEOVER

The Amersham to London coach route run by A&D passed to the Green Line side of LPTB's business on 4th October 1933. To coincide with the takeover, in November 1933 London Transport issued a timetable almost identical to the type already shown but somewhat deeper in size. A copy of this timetable is held in the London Transport Museum Depot at Acton, it shows it was priced for sale to the public at 1d. Everything about this time table is A&D, only the cover has been changed to show the name "London Transport". Even A&D coach hire is advertised. A list of passenger regulations qualifies the carriage of parcels. Upon payment of a charge a parcel could be handed to the conductor who would convey the parcel to a further fare stage and hand it over if met by someone or it would be taken to the depot for collection. Charges were; up to 1lb – 2d; up to 7lb – 4d; up to 14lb – 8d and a maximum 28lb – 1/-. For some reason this timetable also included population figures for the major towns served by the buses running out of Amersham garage; Chesham's was listed as 8809 and Amersham's as 4221.

By the end of 1934 London Transport introduced a new numbering system for routes across its network. Numbers 300-399 were allocated to Will Randall's area and from 3rd October 1934 the old A&D buses displayed numbers to show what routes they were on. The new numbers are shown in brackets and the old A&D ones as only ever shown in the later printed timetables precede them.

1/2 (362); 3(353); 4(394); 5(369A); 6/10 (305); 7(397); 8(348); 9(359); 16(316); Green Line coach service 17(R); 19(369); 20(398) and 23(396). The old N6 route operated by National became the 336.

A&D Routes 21 and 22 had been withdrawn.

APPENDIX 3 - A&D TICKETS

One has to be over 65 to have any recollection of the time when bus tickets were individually pre-printed with the fare, held firmly in the conductor's wooden ticket rack and then punched on the side edge once purchased. The ticket then finally clipped on the base edge by the inspector if he hopped on your particular bus. Each ticket value had its own colour, sometimes with an advertisement on the back. All this was far more interesting and individual to your journey than the later white paper roll printed and torn off for you. The old tickets were firmer, not as stiff as train tickets, but enough to feel you had been given something for the value of your journey; even if you then left it wedged in the seat frame in front of you when you got off!

Amersham & District adopted the Bell Punch Company ticket system. Originally the Company purchased the punch machines and racks, but in the later years when expansion meant they employed so many more conductors, they rented them direct from the manufacturers. Bell Punch was a British engineering company that produced by far the most popular ticketing system across the country. It had been in use by LGOC for many years and went on to serve London Transport into the 1950's. Bell Punch's daily output of tickets from their Uxbridge factory ran into tens of millions. Their ticket system was simple but effective and of huge value to bus operators like A&D. Each ticket had a unique serial number and the batches of numbers held by the conductor were recorded on his "Day sheets". This allowed the office to calculate the traffic on each vehicle, so that its fleet could be best allocated to return a profit. The Bell Punch clipping system rang a bell every time it punched a fresh ticket and some of the mechanisms also had a revolving counter. The bell ensured the conductor had punched a new ticket, and the small circle cut out fell into a sealed container within the punch body. At the end of a shift the tickets issued should balance against takings and any variance could be checked against the evidence of the clippings from each punch operation. By allocating different colours to each price denomination it allowed both the conductor and the passenger a quick and reliable way of ensuring the correct ticket had been issued. The clipping colour held within the punches body also denoted the value of the ticket issued. A&D management would have selected the colour paper on which each ticket was printed.

It seems that the Company used Bell Punch tickets from the very beginning although in the minute books they are first mentioned on 22nd November 1922 when Brandons store of Chesham ask to advertise on the reverse side and Bell Punch put forward their printing charges to the Company. This arrangement with Brandons became ongoing, although a ticket has been seen that just had "TRAVEL A&D" on its reverse.

A typical Bell Punch machine from the period. The machine had leather carry straps that went over the shoulder or around the neck. Photograph N Lamond

An accompanying period ticket rack complete with sample tickets (not of A&D origin).
Photograph N Lamond

Should you have any old A&D tickets acting as page markers inside Granddad's old books then here are some notes on dating them. Please be aware that the dates the tickets would have been issued may fall outside of the dates given as the company will always want to use up its pre-purchased stock. As you might imagine these tickets are extremely rare survivors and some are in delicate condition. They mostly came in 2½ inch size but some longer 3¾ inch sizes were produced later to cope with more fare stages.

 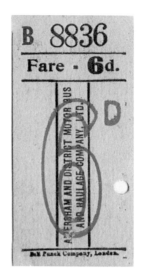 

(Left) This simple 9d ticket would appear to the very earliest in use by the Syndicate as the abbreviated company trading name does not end in Ltd. We might therefore conclude this ticket dates to the period from May-September 1919. The destinations Chesham and High Wycombe refer to the only route in operation by the company at this time. Image courtesy of The Omnibus Society

(Middle) This 6d ticket is likely to come from a period between 1920–1924. The company name is printed in full plus showing it is now registered as a Limited liability entity. Image courtesy of The Omnibus Society

(Right) This 4d ticket remains the same but crucially and seemingly just for a short period in 1925, tickets had a manufactured date printed on them in the bottom right hand corner. In this case 5-25 (May 1925), batches with 10-25 are also known. Image courtesy of the Transport Ticket Society

Image courtesy of the Transport Ticket Society

In the next variation (see above image of 3d fare), the ticket is still very plain but the company name has dropped the "Haulage" element. It seems to have done this without ever actually

94

changing its name officially or registering a new one. It always files its accounts under the full name with "Haulage" in the title. "IN and "OUT" can be seen printed above blank columns on the ticket and punches will be made underneath them to signify in which direction the journey is being taken. The date code in the bottom right has been dropped and just becomes a 4-digit block number sometimes followed by a letter (in this case 2291e but tickets with just 2291 are known), the higher the number the later the printed batch. These block numbers were not unique to each bus operator. The Brandon & Sons advert on the reverse claims they had "FIVE LARGE STORES" this was before the company moved to their large department store on The Broadway at the end of 1928. However to confuse matters a little, tickets with block number 2291 have been seen with the Brandon's advert for 25,000 feet of showrooms as shown on the reverse of the next but one example.

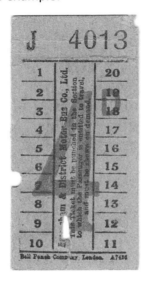

(Left image) This post 1st January 1931 ticket was issued on the new A&D London express coach service that originally started from Chesham but after a few months was restricted to start only from Amersham. This is the first ticket we see from the company to contain fare stages listed. It is quite possible that the tickets originally printed with the Chesham fare stage continued to be used. This ticket has the block number A1439. Image courtesy of The Omnibus Society

(Middle and right images) Later still all the tickets started to bear "Fare Stage" numbering. The A&D minute books record on 24th February 1932 "The Bell Punch Company charge for printing fare stages on all tickets accepted." With the exclusion of the Express Coach Service tickets, this probably means they had never printed fare stages before and so all tickets found with stage numbers down each side are more than likely post February 1932 in date. It seems unlikely that prior to this they had some printed with stage numbers and some without as that would not make for interchange ability between routes. The wording in the centre of the ticket is also interesting as it says "This ticket must be punched in the section to which the Passenger is entitled to travel, and must be shown on demand," as we will see in the next example this rule changes. The code in the bottom right is A7435, later batches have letters higher in the alphabet. Finally the advert for Brandon's has changed and this should reflect that by this time the company has moved to their final departmental store type premises on Chesham Broadway. Image courtesy of the Transport Ticket Society

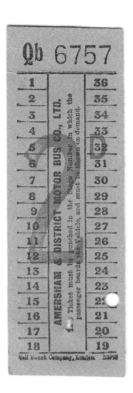

This final 1933 variant of the Company's tickets depicts a longer version to incorporate more fare stages that would be needed on longer journeys. Longer tickets such as this were also held in the same wooden rack. The code to the bottom right starts B followed by 4 digits and the wording down the middle changes to "This ticket must be punched in the Stage Number in which the passenger boards the vehicle, and must be shown on demand." So as we can see this is opposite to the punching requirements of a year or so earlier. Later tickets with batch numbers such as this one come in the shorter standard size ticket as well.

Image courtesy of the Transport Ticket Society

When a conductor punched a ticket he had no guide on his machine to inform him of where to slide the ticket into to achieve the correct hole punch, this was made possible only with experience and holding his thumbnail in a pre-determined position to achieve a punched hole in the required fare stage.

Bell Punch tickets provide the happiest ending to our A&D story........

The punched out pieces of ticket were sometimes known as "confetti" by conductors and even got used as such at busman's weddings.

Going off with a hoot!

THE END

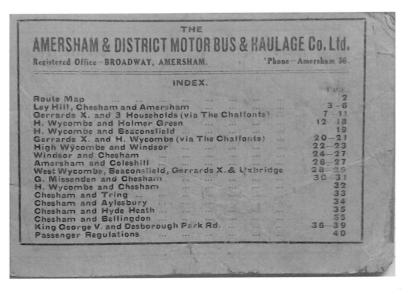

The pleasures of open-top motoring.
'Pride of Bucks' charabancs on route to Eastbourne, 1928.
J CHAPMAN COLLECTION

AMERSHAM & DISTRICT MOTOR BUS Cᵒ. Lᵀᴰ.

In 1919 a group of local entrepreneurs founded the first motor bus
services in and around Amersham and Chesham. The impact they had
on the community was profound and in fourteen years the local bus
moved from novelty to normality.

Research has been undertaken extracting the Company's history
from their accounts, their preserved minute books, contemporary letters to
the press, and material handed down by people who worked for the Company.
Local social history back stories, both sentimental and sad,
add to this fascinating account. Delve into the struggles of a fledgling
business and discover how it finally grew to become one of the largest
independent operators on the outskirts of London.

Lavishly illustrated, mainly with never before published photographs.
In these visions of a lost England you may even catch a glimpse
of your ancestors out enjoying themselves.

ISBN 978-0-9554707-9-0

9 780955 470790

Published by Hawkes Design & Publishing Ltd, Chesham
Cover illustration by Mary Casserley

UK £14.99